Competing Against Luck

ALSO BY THE AUTHORS

ALSO BY CLAYTON M. CHRISTENSEN

The Innovator's Dilemma
Innovation and the General Manager
The Innovator's Solution
Seeing What's Next
The Innovator's Prescription
Disrupting Class
The Innovator's DNA
The Innovative University
The Power of Everyday Missionaries

ALSO BY CLAYTON M. CHRISTENSEN AND KAREN DILLON

How Will You Measure Your Life? (with James Allworth)

ALSO BY KAREN DILLON

HBR Guide to Office Politics

ALSO BY DAVID S. DUNCAN

Building a Growth Factory (with Scott D. Anthony)

Competing Against Luck

THE STORY OF INNOVATION
AND CUSTOMER CHOICE

Clayton M. Christensen

TADDY HALL, KAREN DILLON,
AND DAVID S. DUNCAN

HARPER
BUSINESS

An Imprint of HarperCollins*Publishers*

HarperCollins books may be purchased for educational, business, or sales promotional use. For information, please email the Special Markets Department at SPsales@harpercollins.com.

FIRST EDITION

Library of Congress Cataloging-in-Publication Data has been applied for.

ISBN 978-0-06-243561-3

International ISBN: 978-0-06-256523-5

16 17 18 19 20   RRD   10 9 8 7 6 5 4 3 2 1

CONTENTS

Section 2: The Hard Work—and Payoff—of Applying Jobs Theory

So where are all these jobs just waiting to be discovered—and how do you find them? The solution lies not in the tools you're using, but in what you are looking for and how you piece your observations together.

Customers can't always articulate what they want—their motivations are more complex and their pathways to purchase more elaborate than they can describe. But you can get to the bottom of it. What they "**hire**"—and equally important, what they "**fire**"—tells an important story.

How can you make sure your solution gets "hired" for the job? That involves more than creating a product with the right features and functionality. Truly responding to a Job to Be Done requires enabling the right experiences for your customers. And for that, customers are willing to pay a premium price.

Section 3: The Jobs to Be Done Organization

Organizations typically structure themselves around function or business unit or geography—but true competitive advantage is built when companies optimize around the job. Integrating internal capabilities and processes that nail a job is the mechanism by which companies can truly differentiate their product or service.

CHAPTER 8: KEEPING YOUR EYE ON THE JOB   177

Even great companies can veer off course in nailing the job for their customers—and focus on nailing a job for themselves. That's because companies fall into believing fallacies about the data they generate about their products: the Fallacy of Active Versus Passive Data, the Fallacy of Surface Growth, and the Fallacy of Conforming Data.

CHAPTER 9: THE JOBS-FOCUSED ORGANIZATION   197

A well-articulated job provides a kind of "commander's intent," obviating the need for micromanagement because employees at all levels understand and are motivated by how the work they do fits into a larger process to help customers get their jobs done. Here's how that works at organizations such as the Mayo Clinic, the Consumer Financial Protection Bureau (CFPB), OnStar, and *Deseret News*—to name just a few.

CHAPTER 10: FINAL OBSERVATIONS ABOUT THE THEORY OF JOBS 221

For far too long, we've allowed ourselves to believe that successful innovation is the result of luck. It's time to topple that paradigm. We've spent twenty years gathering evidence showing that you can put your time, energy, and resources into creating competitive advantage through products and services that you can predict, in advance, that customers will be eager to hire. Leave relying on luck to the other guys.

Why You Should Hire This Book

This is a book about progress.

Yes, it's a book about innovation—and how to get better at it. But at its core, this book is about the struggles we all face to make progress in our lives.

If you're like many entrepreneurs and managers, the word "progress" might not spring to mind when you're trying to innovate. Instead you obsess about creating the perfect product with just the right combination of features and benefits to appeal to customers. Or you try to continually fine-tune your existing products so they're more profitable or differentiated from your competitors'. You *think* you know just what your customers would like, but in reality, it can feel pretty hit or miss. Place enough bets and—with a bit of luck—something will work out.

But that doesn't have to be the case, not when you truly understand what *causes* consumers to make the choices they do. Innovation can be far more predictable—and far more profitable—but only if you think about it differently. It's about *progress*, not products. So if you are tired of throwing yourself and your organization into well-intended innovation efforts that routinely underwhelm; if you want to create products and services that you know, in advance, customers will not only be eager to buy, but willing to pay a *premium price* for; if you want to compete—and win—against those relying on luck to successfully innovate, then read on. This book is about helping *you* make progress, too.

GETTING BETTER AND BETTER AT THE WRONG THINGS

For as long as I can remember, innovation has been a top priority—and a top frustration—for companies around the world. In a recent McKinsey poll, 84 percent of global executives acknowledged that innovation is extremely important to their growth strategies, yet a staggering 94 percent were unsatisfied with their own innovation performance. Most people would agree that the *vast majority* of innovations fall far short of ambitions, a fact that has remained unchanged for decades.

On paper, this makes no sense. Companies have never had more sophisticated tools and techniques at their disposal—and there are more resources than ever deployed in reaching innovation goals. In 2015, according to an article in *strategy + business*,[1] one thousand publicly held companies spent $680 *billion* on research and development alone, a 5.1 percent increase over the previous year.

And businesses have never known more about their customers. The big data revolution has greatly increased the variety, volume, and velocity of data collection, along with the sophistication of the analytical tools applied to it. Hopes for this data trove are higher than ever. "Correlation is enough,"[2] then-*Wired* editor in chief Chris Anderson famously declared in 2008. We can, he implied, solve innovation problems by the sheer brute force of the data deluge. Ever since Michael Lewis chronicled the Oakland A's unlikely success in *Moneyball* (who *knew* on-base percentage was a better indicator of offensive success than batting averages?), organizations have been trying to find the *Moneyball* equivalent of customer data that will lead to innovation success. Yet few have.

Innovation processes in many companies are structured and disciplined, and the talent applying them is highly skilled. There are careful stage-gates, rapid iterations, and checks and balances built into most organizations' innovation processes. Risks are carefully calculated and mitigated. Principles like six-sigma have pervaded innovation process design so we now have precise measurements and strict requirements for new products to meet at each stage of their development. From the outside, it looks like companies have mastered an awfully precise, scientific process.

But for most of them, innovation is still painfully hit or miss. And worst of all, all this activity gives the *illusion* of progress, without actually causing it. Companies are spending exponentially more to achieve only modest incremental innovations while completely missing the mark on the breakthrough innovations critical to long-term, sustainable growth. As Yogi Berra famously observed: "We're lost, but we're making good time!"

What's gone so wrong?

Here is the fundamental problem: the masses and masses of data that companies accumulate are not organized in a way that enables them to reliably predict which ideas will succeed. Instead the data is along the lines of "this customer looks like that one," "this product has similar performance attributes as that one," and "these people behaved the same way in the past," or "68 percent of customers say they prefer version A over version B." None of that data, however, actually tells you *why* customers make the choices that they do.

Let me illustrate. Here I am, Clayton Christensen. I'm sixty-four years old. I'm six feet eight inches tall. My shoe size is sixteen. My wife and I have sent all our children off to college. I live in a suburb of Boston and drive a Honda minivan to work. I have a lot of other characteristics and attributes. But these characteristics have not yet *caused* me to go out and buy the *New York Times* today. There might be a correlation between some of these characteristics and the propensity of customers to purchase the *Times*. But those attributes don't *cause* me to buy that paper—or *any* other product.

If a company doesn't understand *why* I might choose to "hire" its product in certain circumstances—and why I might choose something else in others—its data[3] about me or people like me[4] is unlikely to help it create any new innovations for me. It's seductive to believe that we can see important patterns and cross-references in our data sets, but that doesn't mean one thing actually caused the other. As Nate Silver, author of *The Signal and the Noise: Why So Many Predictions Fail—But Some Don't,* points out, "ice cream sales and forest fires are correlated because both occur more often in the summer heat. But there is no causation; you don't light a patch of the Montana brush on fire when you buy a pint of Häagen-Dazs."

Of course, it's no surprise that correlation isn't the same as causality. But although most organizations know that, I don't think they act as if there is a difference. They're *comfortable* with correlation. It allows managers to sleep at night.

But correlation does not reveal the one thing that matters most in innovation—the causality behind *why* I might purchase a particular solution. Yet few innovators frame their primary challenge around the discovery of a *cause.* Instead, they focus on how they can make their products better, more profitable, or differentiated from the competition.

As W. Edwards Deming, the father of the quality movement that transformed manufacturing, once said: "If you do not know how to ask the right question, you discover nothing." After decades of watching great companies fail over and over again, I've come to the conclusion that there is, indeed, a better question to ask: *What job did you hire that product to do?*

For me, this is a neat idea. When we buy a product, we essentially "hire" something to get a job done. If it does the job well, when we are confronted with the same job, we hire that same product again. And if the product does a crummy job, we "fire" it and look around for something else we might hire to solve the problem.

Every day stuff happens to us. Jobs arise in our lives that we need to get done. Some jobs are little ("pass the time while wait-ing in line"), some are big ("find a more fulfilling career"). Some surface unpredictably ("dress for an out-of-town business meeting after the airline lost my suitcase"), some regularly ("pack a healthy, tasty lunch for my daughter to take to school"). Other times we know they're coming. When we realize we have a job to do, we reach out and pull something into our lives to get the job done. I might, for example, choose to buy the *New York Times* because I have a job to fill my time while waiting for a doctor's appoint-ment and I don't want to read the boring magazines available in the lobby. Or perhaps because I'm a basketball fan and it's March Madness time. It's only when a job arises in my life that the *Times* can solve for me that I'll choose to hire the paper to do it. Or per-haps I have it delivered to my door so that my neighbors think I'm informed—and nothing about their ZIP code or median house-hold income will tell the *Times* that either.

This core insight emerged in the course I teach at Harvard Business School, but has subsequently been refined and shaped over the past two decades by numerous conversations with my co-authors, trusted colleagues, collaborators, and thought-leaders. It's been validated and proven in the work of some of the world's most respected business leaders and innovators—Amazon's Jeff Bezos and Intuit's Scott Cook, for example—as well as in the founding of highly successful entrepreneurial ventures in recent years. Who would have imagined that a service that makes travelers pay to stay in a stranger's spare bedroom would be valued at more than Marriott, Starwood, or Wyndham Worldwide? Airbnb did it. The videos that Sal Khan made to teach math to his young cousin were, by his description, "cheaper and crappier" than many other educational videos already online, but they now enable millions of students all over the world to learn at their own pace.

These innovations weren't aimed at jumping on the latest trends or rolling out another new flavor to boost sales. They weren't created to add more bells and whistles to an existing product so the company could charge customers more. They were conceived, developed, and launched into the market with a clear understanding of how these products would help consumers make the progress they were struggling to achieve. When you have a job to be done and there isn't a good solution, "cheaper and crappier" is better than nothing. Imagine the potential of something truly great.

This book is not focused on celebrating past innovation successes, however. It's about something much more important to *you*: creating and predicting new ones.

The foundation of our thinking is the Theory of Jobs to Be Done, which focuses on deeply understanding your customers' *struggle for progress* and then creating the right solution and attendant set of experiences to ensure you solve your customers' jobs well, every time. "Theory" may conjure up images of ivory tower musings, but I assure you that it is the most practical and useful business tool we can offer you. Good theory helps us understand "how" and "why." It helps us make sense of how the world works and predict the consequences of our decisions and our actions. Jobs Theory[5], we believe, can move companies beyond hoping that correlation is enough to the causal mechanism of successful innovation.

Innovation may never be a perfect science, but that's not the point. We have the ability to make innovation a reliable engine for growth, an engine based on a clear understanding of causality, rather than simply casting seeds in the hopes of one day harvesting some fruit.

The Theory of Jobs to Be Done is the product of some very real-world insights and experiences. I've asked my coauthors to work with me on this book in part because they've been using Jobs Theory in their everyday work for years and have much experience bringing the theory into the practical realm of innovation. Together we have shaped, refined, and polished the theory, along with the thoughts and contributions of many trusted colleagues and business leaders, whose work and insights we'll feature throughout this book.

My coauthor **Taddy Hall** was in my first class at Harvard Business School and he and I have collaborated on projects throughout the years, including coauthoring with Intuit founder Scott Cook the *Harvard Business Review* (*HBR*) article "Marketing Malpractice" that first debuted the Jobs to Be Done theory in the pages of *HBR*. He's currently a principal at the Cambridge Group (part of the Nielsen Company) and leader of the Nielsen Breakthrough Innovation Project. As such, he has worked closely with some of the world's leading companies, including many of those mentioned throughout this book. More important, he's used Jobs Theory in his innovation advisory work for years.

Karen Dillon is the former editor of *Harvard Business Review* and my coauthor on *How Will You Measure Your Life?* You'll see her perspective as a longtime senior manager in media organizations struggling to get innovation right reflected in this book. Throughout our collaboration, she has seen her role as that of a proxy for you, the reader. She is also one of my most trusted allies in helping bridge the worlds of academia and practitioners.

David S. Duncan is a senior partner at Innosight, a consulting firm I cofounded in 2000. He's a leading thinker and adviser to senior executives on innovation strategy and growth, helping them to navigate disruptive change, create sustainable growth, and transform their organizations to thrive for the long term. The clients he's worked with tell me they've completely changed the way they think about their business and transformed their culture to be truly focused on customer jobs. (One client even named a conference room after him.) Over the past decade, his work in helping to develop and implement Jobs Theory has made him one of its most knowledgeable and innovative practitioners.

Throughout the book, we've primarily chosen to use the

first-person "I" simply to make it more accessible for readers. But we have written this book as true partners; it's very much the product of a collaborative "we" and our collective expertise.

Finally, a quick roadmap of the book: Section 1 provides an introduction to Jobs Theory as the causal mechanism fueling successful innovation. Section 2 shifts from theory to practice and describes the hard work of applying Jobs Theory in the messy tumult of the real world. Section 3 outlines the organizational and leadership implications, challenges, and payoffs posed by focusing on Jobs to Be Done. To facilitate your journey through each of these sections of the book and to maximize its value to you, at the outset of each chapter we've included "The Big Idea" as well as a brief recap of "Takeaways." At the end of chapters 2 to 9, we've included a list of questions for leaders to ask their organizations, with the aim of helping executives start to put these ideas into practice.

Our preference is to *show* through examples more than to *tell* in the form of assertion or opinion. As is true in discovering Jobs to Be Done, we find that stories are a more powerful mechanism for teaching you how to think, rather than just telling you what to think—stories that we'll weave throughout the book. Our hope is that in the process of reading this book, you will come away with a new understanding of how to improve your own innovation success.

WHAT JOB DID YOU HIRE THAT PRODUCT TO DO?

Organizations around the world have devoted countless resources— including time, energy, and mindshare of top executives—to the challenge of innovation. And they have, naturally, optimized what they do for efficiency. But if all this effort is aimed at answering the wrong questions, it's sitting on a very tenuous foundation.

As W. Edwards Deming is also credited with observing, every process is perfectly designed to deliver the results it gets. If we believe that innovation is messy and imperfect and unknowable, we build processes that operationalize those beliefs. And that's what many companies have done: unwittingly designed innovation processes that perfectly churn out mediocrity. They spend time and money compiling data-rich models that make them masters of description but failures at prediction.

We don't have to settle for that. There is a better question to ask—one that can help us understand the causality underlying a customer's decision to pull a new product into his or her life. ***What job did you hire that product to do?*** The good news is that if you build your foundation on the pursuit of understanding your customers' jobs, your strategy will no longer need to rely on luck. In fact, you'll be *competing against luck* when others are still counting on it. You'll see the world with new eyes. Different competitors, different priorities, and most important, different results. You can leave hit-or-miss innovation behind.

NOTES

1. Jaruzelski, Barry, Kevin Schwartz, and Volker Staack. "Innovation's New World Order." *strategy+business*, October 2015.

2. Anderson, Chris. "The End of Theory: The Data Deluge Makes the Scientific Method Obsolete." *Wired*, June 23, 2008.

3. My son Spencer was a really good pitcher in our town's Little League. I can still see his big hands wrapped around the ball, his composure when a tough batter was at the plate, the way he'd regroup after each pitch with renewed focus. He was unflappable in some very big moments. Someplace there is data that will tell you the number of games he won and lost, how many balls and strikes he threw, and so on. But none of that will ever tell you why. Data is not the phenomenon. It represents the phenomenon, but not very well.

4. During the 1950s, the US Air Force realized that pilots were having trouble controlling their planes. As recounted by Todd Rose, director of the Mind, Brain, and Education program at the Harvard Graduate School of Education, in *The End of Average*, the Air Force first assumed the problem was poor training or pilot error. But it turned out that wasn't the problem at all. The cockpits had a design flaw: they had been built around the "average" pilot in the 1920s. Since it was obvious that Americans had gotten bigger since then, the Air Force decided to update their measurements of the "average pilot." That involved measuring more than four thousand pilots of nearly a dozen dimensions of size related to how they'd fit into a cockpit. If those cockpits could be redesigned to fit the average pilot in the 1950s, the problem should be solved, the Air Force concluded. So how many pilots actually fell into the definition of average after this enormous undertaking? None, Rose reports. Every single pilot had what Rose called a "jagged profile." Some had long legs, while others had long arms. The height never corresponded with the same chest or head size. And so on. The revised cockpits designed for everyone actually fit no one. When the Air Force finally swept aside

the baseline assumptions, the adjustable seat was born. There's no such thing as "average" in the real world. And innovating toward "average" is doomed to fail. Rose, Todd. *The End of Average: How We Succeed in a World That Values Sameness*. New York: HarperCollins, 2015.

5. Throughout the book, we use the Theory of Jobs to Be Done and Jobs Theory interchangeably. They mean the same thing.

SECTION I

AN INTRODUCTION TO JOBS THEORY

We're lost, but we're making good time!

—YOGI BERRA

CHAPTER I

The Milk Shake Dilemma

THE BIG IDEA

Why is innovation so hard to predict—and sustain? Because we haven't been asking the right questions. Despite the success and enduring utility of disruption as a model of competitive response, it does not tell you where to look for new opportunities. It doesn't provide a road map for where or how a company should innovate to undermine established leaders or create new markets. But the Theory of Jobs to Be Done does.

Why is success so hard to sustain?

That question nagged at me for years. In the early years of my career, I had the opportunity to work closely with many companies that were in trouble, first as a consultant for Boston Consulting Group and then as the CEO of my own company, CPS Technologies, a company I founded with several MIT professors to make products out of a set of advanced materials they had developed. And I witnessed firsthand how a lot of smart people were unable to fix the problems of once-great companies. At that same time, I watched the rise of a local Boston company, Digital Equipment

Corporation (DEC), as it became one of the most admired in the world. Whenever you read explanations about why it was so successful, inevitably its success was attributed to the brilliance of the company's management team. Then about 1988 Digital Equipment fell off the cliff and began to unravel very quickly. When you then read explanations about why it had stumbled so badly, it was always attributed to the ineptitude of the management team, the same folks running the company who had earned unfettered praise for so long.

For a while, the way I framed it was, "Gee, how could smart people get so stupid so fast?" And that is the way most people accepted the demise of DEC: somehow the same management team that had its act together at one point was out of its league at another. But the "stupid manager" hypothesis really didn't hold up when you considered that almost every minicomputer company in the world collapsed in unison.

So when I returned to Harvard Business School (HBS) for my doctorate, I brought with me a set of puzzles to try to answer as an academic. Was there something other than bad management that played a key role in the demise of these great companies? Were they only successful in the first place because they'd gotten lucky in some way? Had these incumbents fallen behind the times, relied on antiquated products, and just lost their step as more nimble competitors appeared? Was the creation of new successful products and businesses intrinsically a crapshoot?

But after diving into my research, I realized that my initial assumptions were wrong. What I found was that even the best professional managers—doing all the right things and following all the best advice—could lead their companies all the way to the top of their markets and then fall straight off a cliff after arriving there. Nearly all the incumbents in the industry I studied—disk drive manufacturers—were eventually beaten by new entrants with cheaper and initially far inferior offerings—what I called "disruptive innovations."

That work led to my theory of disruptive innovation,[1] which explains the phenomenon by which an innovation transforms an existing market or sector by introducing simplicity, convenience, accessibility, and affordability where complication and high cost have become the status quo—eventually completely redefining the industry.

At its core, it's a theory of *competitive response to an innovation.* It explains and predicts the behavior of companies in danger of being disrupted, providing insight into the mistakes incumbent leaders make in response to what initially seem to be minuscule threats. It also provides a way for incumbents to predict what innovations on the horizon are likely to be the greatest disruptive threats. But over the past two decades, the theory of disruption has been interpreted and misapplied so broadly as to mean anything that's clever, new, and ambitious.

But the theory of disruptive innovation does not tell you where to look for new opportunities. It doesn't predict or explain how, specifically, a company should innovate to undermine the established leaders or where to create new markets. It doesn't tell you how to avoid the frustration of hit-and-miss innovation—leaving your fate to luck. It doesn't tell you how to create products and services that customers will want to buy—and predict which new products will succeed.

But the Theory of Jobs to Be Done does.

MILK SHAKES IN THE MORNING

In the mid-1990s, two consultants from Detroit asked if they could visit my office at Harvard Business School to learn more about my then newly published theory of disruptive innovation. Bob Moesta and his partner at the time, Rick Pedi, were developing a niche business advising bakeries and snack-food companies on developing new products that people would predictably buy.

As we discussed the theory of disruption, I could see that it predicted very clearly what the established companies in the market would do in the face of an impending disruption from small bakers and snack-food companies. In that regard, it offered a clear statement of cause and effect. But as we talked, it became apparent that the theory of disruption did not provide a roadmap for their clients. The theory of disruption does not offer a clear and complete causal explanation of what a company should do offensively to be successful: if you do *this* and not *that,* you will win. In fact, I realized that even if a company has the intent to disrupt a vulnerable incumbent, the odds of creating *exactly* the right product or service to achieve that are probably less than 25 percent. If that.

For years, I'd been focused on understanding why great companies fail, but I realized I had never really thought about the reverse problem: *How do successful companies know how to grow?*

It wasn't for months that I finally had an answer. Moesta shared with me a project for a fast-food chain: how to sell more milk shakes. The chain had spent months studying the problem in incredible detail. It had brought in customers that fit the profile of the quintessential milk shake consumer and peppered them with questions: "Can you tell us how we can improve our milk shakes so you'd buy more of them? Do you want it cheaper? Chunkier? Chewier? Chocolatier?" Even when customers explained what they thought they would like, it was hard to know exactly what to do. The chain tried many things in response to the customer feedback, innovations specifically intended to satisfy the highest number of potential milk shake buyers. Within months, something notable happened: Nothing. After all the marketers' efforts, there was no change in sales of the chain's milk shake category.

So we thought of approaching the question in a totally different way: *I wonder what job arises in people's lives that causes them to come to this restaurant to "hire" a milk shake?*

I thought that was an interesting way to think about the problem. Those customers weren't simply buying a product, they were hiring the milk shake to perform a specific *job* in their lives. What *causes* us to buy products and services is the stuff that happens to us all day, every day. We all have jobs we need to do that arise in our day-to-day lives and when we do, we hire products or services to get these jobs done.

Armed with that perspective, the team found itself standing in a restaurant for eighteen hours one day, watching people: What time did people buy these milk shakes? What were they wearing? Were they alone? Did they buy other food with it? Did they drink it in the restaurant or drive off with it?

It turned out that a surprising number of milk shakes were sold before 9:00 a.m. to people who came into the fast-food restaurant alone. It was almost always the only thing they bought. They didn't stop to drink it there; they got into their cars and drove off with it. So we asked them: "Excuse me, please, but I have to sort out this puzzle. What job were you trying to do for yourself that caused you to come here and hire that milk shake?"

At first the customers themselves had a hard time answering that question until we probed on what else they sometimes hired instead of a milk shake. But it soon became clear that the early-morning customers all had the same job to do: they had a long and boring ride to work. They needed something to keep the commute interesting. They weren't really hungry yet, but they knew that in a couple of hours, they'd face a midmorning stomach rumbling. It turned out that there were a lot of competitors for this job, but none of them did the job perfectly. "I hire bananas sometimes. But take my word for it: don't do bananas. They are gone too quickly—and you'll be hungry again by midmorning," one told us. Doughnuts were too crumbly and left the customers' fingers sticky, making a mess on their clothes and the steering wheel as they tried to eat and drive. Bagels were often dry and tasteless—forcing people to drive their cars with their knees while they spread cream cheese and jam on the bagels. Another commuter confessed, "One time I hired a

Snickers bar. But I felt so guilty about eating candy for breakfast that I never did it again." But a milk shake? It was the best of the lot. It took a long time to finish a thick milk shake with that thin straw. And it was substantial enough to ward off the looming midmorning hunger attack. One commuter effused, "This milk shake. It is so thick! It easily takes me twenty minutes to suck it up through that thin straw. Who cares what the ingredients are—I don't. All I know is that I'm full all morning. And it fits right here in my cup holder"—as he held up his empty hand. It turns out that the milk shake does the job better than any of the competitors— which, in the customers' minds, are not just milk shakes from other chains but bananas, bagels, doughnuts, breakfast bars, smoothies, coffee, and so on.

As the team put all these answers together and looked at the diverse profiles of these people, another thing became clear: what these milk shake buyers had in common had nothing to do with their individual demographics. Rather, they all shared a common job they needed to get done in the morning.

"Help me stay awake and occupied while I make my morning commute more fun." We had the answer!

Alas, it wasn't that simple.

Turns out that plenty of milk shakes are purchased in the afternoon and evening, outside of the context of a commute. In those circumstances, the same customers could hire a milk shake for a completely different job. Parents have had to say "no" to their children about any number of things all week long. *No new toy. No, you can't stay up late. No, you can't have a dog!* I recognized that I was one of those dads, searching for a moment to connect with my children. I'd been looking for something innocuous to which I could say "yes"—so I can feel like a kind and loving dad. So I'm standing there in line with my son in the late afternoon and I order my meal. Then my son pauses to look up at me, like only a son can, and asks, "Dad, can I have a milk shake, too?" And the moment has arrived. We're not at home where I promise my wife to limit unhealthy snacks around mealtime. We're in the place where I can finally say "yes" to my son because this is a special occasion. I reach down, put my hand on his shoulder, and say, "Of course, Spence, you can have a milk shake." In that moment, the milk shake isn't competing against a banana or a Snickers bar or a doughnut, like the morning milk shake is. It's competing against stopping at the toy store or my finding time for a game of catch later on.

Think about how different that job is from the commuter's job—and how different the competition is for getting those jobs done. Imagine our fast-food restaurant inviting a dad like me to give feedback in one of its customer surveys, asking the question posed earlier: "How can we improve this milk shake so you buy more of them?" What is that dad going to tell them? Is it the same thing that the morning commuter would say?

The morning job needs a more viscous milk shake, which takes a long time to suck up during the long, boring commute. You might add in chunks of fruit, but not to make it healthy. That's not the reason it's being hired. Instead, fruit or even bits of chocolate would offer a little "surprise" in each sip of the straw and help keep the commute interesting. You could also think about moving the dispensing machine from behind the counter to the front of the counter and providing a swipe card, so morning commuters could dash in, fill a milk shake cup themselves, and rush out again.

In the afternoon, I'm the same person, but in very different circumstances. The afternoon, placate-your-children-and-feel-like-a-good-dad job is very different. Maybe the afternoon milk shake should come in half sizes so it can be finished more quickly and not induce so much guilt in Dad. If this fast-food company had only focused on how to make its product "better" in a general way—thicker, sweeter, bigger—it would have been focusing on the wrong unit of analysis. You have to understand the *job* the customer is trying to do in a specific circumstance. If the company simply tried to average all the responses of the dads and the commuters, it would come up with a one-size-fits-none product that doesn't do either of the jobs well.

And therein lies the "aha."

People hired milk shakes for two very different jobs during the day, in two very different circumstances. Each job has a very different set of competitors—in the morning it was bagels and protein bars and bottles of fresh juice, for example; in the afternoon, milk shakes are competing with a stop at the toy store or rushing home early to shoot a few hoops—and therefore was being evaluated as the best solution according to very different criteria. This implies there is likely *not* just one solution for the fast-food chain seeking to sell more milk shakes. There are two. A one-size-fits-all solution would work for neither.

A RÉSUMÉ FOR MARGARINE

For me, framing innovation challenges through the lens of jobs customers are trying to get done was an exciting breakthrough. It offered what the theory of disruption couldn't: an understanding of what causes customers to pull products or services into their lives.

The jobs perspective made so much sense to me, intuitively, that I was eager to test it with other companies struggling with innovation. That soon came in an unexpected form. It was margarine—what was unglamorously known in the industry as the "yellow fats"—that provided the opportunity. Shortly after we worked through the milk shake dilemma, I was preparing for a visit from Unilever executives to my classroom at Harvard Business School. Among other goals for the week was to discuss innovation in the margarine category, at the time a multibillion-dollar business. Unilever commanded something like 70 percent of the market in the United States. When you have such a large market share and you already have created a wide variety of margarine-type products, it's difficult to see from where growth can possibly come. I was optimistic that Jobs Theory would offer Unilever a chance to rethink its potential for growth, but that's not what happened. In fact, Unilever's dilemma helped me understand why one of the most important principles in innovation—what *causes* customers to make the choices they do—doesn't seem to get traction with most organizations.

Here's how it played out: Inspired by our milk shake insights, my daughter Ann and I sat in our kitchen thinking about what job we might hire margarine to do. In our case, it was often hired to wet the popcorn just enough for the salt to stick. But not nearly as well as the better-tasting butter. So we headed into the field to our local Star Market to see if we could learn more about why people buy this substitute for butter. We were immediately struck by the overwhelming variety of products available. There were something like twenty-one different brands of margarine right next to its nemesis, butter. We thought we understood the basic benefits of margarine: with its lower fat content, it might have been considered healthier at the time.[2] And it was cheaper than butter. Yes, those twenty-one options were slightly different, but those differences seemed focused only on improving an attribute—percentage of fat—that was irrelevant to any job we would hire margarine to do. As we stood there watching which choices people made, we couldn't quite figure out why people would choose one over the other. There was no obvious correlation between the demographic of the shoppers and their choices, as had been the case with milk shakes.

We watched people make their selections and asked ourselves, "What job are we seeing?" The longer we stood there, the clearer it became that the decision wasn't quite as simple as margarine versus butter. Standing in the cold foods aisle, we realized we weren't even seeing all of margarine's possible competitors. Margarine could be hired for the job of "I need something that moistens the crust on my bread so that it is easier to chew." Most margarine and butters are so hard that they tear apart the bread—giving you a big chunk of fat in the middle of the bread that already is easy to chew and doesn't spread well to the periphery where it needs to be moist. Competitors for that job could include butter, cream cheese, olive oil, mayonnaise, and so on, although all are, in my opinion, essentially tasteless.[3] Or was margarine being hired for a completely different job—help me not to burn my food when I'm cooking. Competitors for that job would include Teflon and nonstick cooking spray, products that were in two completely different aisles, neither of which I could see from the cold foods section.

When you consider the market for margarine from the perspective of what it was actually competing with in consumers' minds, new avenues for growth open up. When a customer decides to buy this product versus that product, she has in her mind, a kind of résumé of the competing products that makes it clear which does her job best. Imagine, for example, writing a résumé for every competing product. Butter—the product that we originally thought was margarine's prime competitor—might be hired to flavor food. But it's not always margarine's competitor. You can also write a résumé for Teflon. For olive oil. For mayonnaise. People might hire the same product to do different jobs at different times in their lives—much like the milk shake. Unilever might have had a large share of what marketers have defined as the yellow fats business, but no customer walks into the store saying, "I need to buy something in the yellow fats category." They come in with a specific Job to Be Done.

We may not have correctly identified all the other products margarine was competing with that day in our local grocery store, but one thing became clear: seen through the lens of Jobs to Be Done, the market for margarine was potentially much larger than Unilever may have previously calculated.

I was so sure of the power of this insight that we presented this thinking to the Unilever executives who came to HBS for the executive education program. I suggested that if they could determine all the jobs customers were hiring margarine to do, they might think about how to grow the business differently.

Alas, the conversation did not go well. Perhaps we didn't have the right language at the time to explain our thinking, but the Unilever executives in the room were not moved by what we were trying to say. I actually called an early break and suggested we just move on to a new topic. We didn't revisit the subject of Jobs to Be Done.

I have no doubt that the Unilever executives in the room that day were seasoned, sophisticated leaders. But their tepid response made me wonder how many companies are operating within such fixed assumptions about how to think about innovation that it's difficult to step back and assess whether they're even asking the right questions. Executives are inundated with data about their products. They know market share to the nth degree, how products are selling in different markets, profit margin across hundreds of different items, and so on. But all this data is focused around customers and the product itself—*not* how well the product is solving customers' jobs. Even customer satisfaction metrics, which reveal whether a customer is happy with a product or not, don't give any clues as to how to do the job better. Yet it's how most companies track and measure success.

In the years since the Unilever executives visited Harvard, the yellow fats business (more recently called "spreads") has not fared particularly well. I have only an outsider's perspective, but as far as I can tell, Unilever more or less pursued the same strategy it had pursued for margarine in 1997: it continued to differentiate its products in traditional ways. By the mid-2000s, butter surpassed margarine in American households—in part due to health concerns about the trans fats in margarine.[4] Margarine has yet to recover. By 2013 one analyst went so far as to suggest that Unilever put its spreads category on notice to be fired. "We question whether it's getting to the stage when Unilever needs to start considering disposal in this persistently disappointing category," Graham

Jones, executive director of equity research for consumer staples at Panmure Gordon, wrote. By the end of 2014 Unilever announced its intention to separate its struggling spreads division into a stand-alone company to help stabilize sales in a business that had become a drag on overall growth as margarine fell out of favor with shoppers. By early 2016 the head of Unilever's margarine group was replaced and speculation about Unilever's future in the margarine business was renewed.

By contrast, the global olive oil market is one of the fastest growing in the food industry. Unilever is a world-class company that's done a lot of things right in the past two decades. But I can't help but wonder how a different lens on the competitive landscape may have altered Unilever's path.

JOBS THEORY AND INNOVATION

That experience made me realize that part of the problem is that we're missing the right vocabulary to talk about innovation in ways that help us understand what actually *causes* it to succeed. Innovators are left to mix, match, and often misapply inadequate concepts and terminology designed for other purposes. We're awash in data, frameworks, customer categories, and performance metrics intended for other purposes on the assumption that they're helpful for innovation, too.

As an academic, I fear we must take some of the blame. In business schools we teach myriad forms of analytics—regression, factor analysis, principal components analysis, and conjoint analysis. There are courses on marketing at the bottom of the pyramid and on marketing for not-for-profit organizations. For years, a popular course at HBS was one in which PET brain scanners showed how different advertising images affected the flow of blood in the brain. But we haven't given students in our classrooms and managers on the front lines of innovation the right tools, forcing them to borrow and adapt tools intended for other purposes. And in spite of all this, a lot of innovation effort is ultimately assumed to be a consequence of good luck anyway. How often do you hear a success dismissed as simply the right product at the right time? We can do better than that.

I've spent the last two decades trying to refine the Theory of Jobs to Be Done so that it actually helps executives transform innovation. There are a handful of aficionados who have also focused on Jobs Theory, including the partners at Innosight, a strategy-and-growth consulting firm I founded, and Bob Moesta, whose consulting work now focuses exclusively on Jobs Theory. Innosight senior partner David Duncan and Nielsen's Taddy Hall, two of my coauthors on this book, have both used the theory on an almost daily basis with their clients for years. Together, with the help of colleagues and thought-leaders whose perspective we deeply value, we've shaped the theory that we offer here.

We recognize that there are other voices in the developing "Jobs" space and we welcome that conversation. We might all use slightly different words or emphasize slightly different methods of divining the right solutions for jobs, but we hope this book serves to create a common language around the Theory of Jobs to Be Done so that we can strengthen and improve our collective understanding. At its heart, we believe Jobs Theory provides a powerful way of understanding the *causal mechanism* of customer behavior, an understanding that, in turn, is the most fundamental driver of innovation success.

If you consider some of the most surprising innovation successes in recent years, I'll wager that all of them had implicitly or explicitly identified a Job to Be Done—and offered a product or service that performed that job extremely well. Consider the exponential success of Uber, which has succeeded remarkably despite staunch resistance from entrenched, government-backed competitors. As we'll discuss later in the book, what Uber did was recognize and then nail the unsatisfactorily filled job of urban transportation.

It is always tempting to look at innovation success stories and retrofit the explanation for why it succeeded (though I do believe that a well-defined job was implicitly at the core of most innovation success stories in history). But we don't intend to rely on looking at those successes in hindsight. Instead, we will illustrate how the theory (which we'll explain fully in the chapters ahead) can fundamentally improve innovation—making it both predictable and replicable through real-world examples of companies that consciously used Jobs to Be Done to create breakthrough innovations. The value of Jobs Theory *to you* is not in explaining past successes, but in predicting new ones.

You may be asking, if Jobs Theory is so powerful, why aren't more companies using it already? First, as we'll explain later, the definition of what we mean by a job is highly specific and precise. It's not an all-purpose catchphrase for something that a customer wants or needs. It's not just a new buzzword. Finding and understanding jobs—and then creating the right product or service to solve them—takes work.

There are multiple layers to the Jobs Theory construct to ensure that you create products that customers will not only want to buy, but also products they're willing to pay premium prices for, as we'll discuss throughout this book. Identifying and understanding the Job to Be Done is key, but it's just the beginning.

After you've uncovered and understood the job, you need to translate those insights into a blueprint to guide the development of products and services that customers will love. This involves creating the right set of *experiences* that accompany your product or service in solving the job (as we'll discuss more fully in chapter 6). And finally you have to ensure that you have integrated your company's internal capabilities and processes to nail the job consistently (chapter 7). Creating the right experiences and then integrating around them to solve a job, is critical for competitive advantage. That's because while it may be easy for competitors to copy products, it's difficult for them to copy *experiences* that are *well integrated* into your company's processes.

But to do all this well takes a holistic effort—from the original insight that led to the identification of the job all the way through to the product finding its way into the hands of a consumer—involving the decisions and influence of virtually *everyone* in the company. Even great innovators who are crystal clear on the jobs their customers are hiring their products and services to do can easily lose their way. Pressures of return on net assets (RONA), well-intended efficiency drives, and decisions made every day on the front lines of business can have a profound effect on the successful (or unsuccessful) delivery of a great solution to a job (as we'll discuss in chapter 8). There are so many ways to stumble on the journey. But the payoff for getting it right is enormous.

Most of the world's most successful innovators see problems through a different lens from the rest of us. Why didn't Hertz come up with a Zipcar-like product first? Kodak came close to creating a kind of Facebook product long before Mark Zuckerberg did. Major yogurt manufacturers understood that there might be a demand for Greek yogurt well before Chobani founder Hamdi Ulukaya launched what is now a $1 billion business. AT&T introduced a "picture phone" at the 1964 World's Fair, decades before Apple's iPhone. Instead of looking at the way the world is and assuming that's the best predictor of the way the world will be, great innovators push themselves to look beyond entrenched assumptions to wonder if, perhaps, there was a better way.

And there is.

CHAPTER TAKEAWAYS

- Disruption, a theory of competitive response to an innovation, provides valuable insights to managers seeking to navigate threats and opportunities. But it leaves unanswered the critical question of *how* a company should innovate to consistently grow. It does not provide guidance on specifically *where* to look for new opportunities, or specifically *what* products and services you should create that customers will want to buy.

• This book introduces the Theory of Jobs to Be Done to answer these questions and provide clear guidance for companies looking to grow through innovation. At its heart, Jobs Theory explains *why* customers pull certain products and services into their lives: they do this to resolve highly important, unsatisfied jobs that arise. And this, in turn, explains why some innovations are successful and others are not.

• Jobs Theory not only provides a powerful guide for innovation, but also frames competition in a way that allows for real differentiation and long-term competitive advantage, provides a common language for organizations to understand customer behavior, and even enables leaders to articulate their company's purpose with greater precision.

NOTES

1. Christensen, Clayton M. *The Innovator's Dilemma: When New Technologies Cause Great Firms to Fail*. Boston: Harvard Business School Press, 1997.

2. A preponderance of evidence has since revealed the adverse effects of trans fats (something my daughter and I were admittedly unaware of at the time). Jobs Theory helps you understand why your customers make the choices that they make—not whether you *should* offer a solution to their job. Cigarettes, for example, could be hired to satisfy an array of jobs, but are not good for the health of the customer. Ethical choices are, of course, equally important to get right.

3. Maybe "tasteless" is a bit unfair. My family recently spent a long weekend in Bar Harbor, Maine—one of the lobster capitals of the world. At every corner there seems to be another lobster shack of some sort. As seafood lovers, we thought this was heaven! We sat down at one lobster shack and I spotted "lobster burgers" on the menu. Now, I love hamburgers. And I love lobsters. So I thought two-in-one was neat. But when they handed me my lobster burger, it was simply a lobster tail in a bun. No dressing. No tartar sauce. No butter. When I took a bite, I had a surprising revelation: the lobster itself had absolutely no taste! The reason it usually tastes so good is that ordering lobster gives you license to drown it in butter. It's the butter that tastes good, not the lobster. This experience made me think: how many other "substrates" was I eating, unaware that they themselves had absolutely no taste! I realized all of these things—the substrates—are essentially platforms upon which you build wonderful flavors and textures. So perhaps the industry is cut the wrong way! You could sell substrates, but then profitably sell "augmentation" stock as well.

4. The American Heart Association currently recommends buying soft, trans fat–free spreads instead of regular butter or stick margarine.

CHAPTER 2

Progress, Not Products

THE BIG IDEA

The more we think we know, the more frustrating it becomes that we keep getting innovation wrong. But you don't have to leave your fate to luck. Successful innovations don't result from understanding your customers' traits, creating jazzy new bells and whistles for your products, catching hot trends, or emulating your competitors. To elevate innovation from hit-or-miss to predictable, you have to understand the underlying causal mechanism—the progress a consumer is trying to make in particular circumstances. Welcome to the Theory of Jobs to Be Done.

When we hear the name Louis Pasteur, most of us recall that the French chemist had something to do with making milk safer to drink. In perhaps the ultimate symbol of his impact on the world, his name has given rise to a verb: to "pasteurize." But Pasteur is responsible for so much more.

To understand how revolutionary Pasteur's contributions were, consider the previously popular ideas that attempted to explain why people got sick. For nearly two thousand years, the medical profession believed that four different bodily fluids—blood, phlegm, yellow bile, and black bile—dominated the health and moods of people. When they were in harmony, all was right with the world. When they were out of sync, people fell ill or into "bad humor." The theory was known as humorism. Doctors were never quite certain what caused imbalance among these humors—ideas ranged from seasons to diet to evil spirits. So they experimented by trial and error to restore the necessary harmony of fluids—often with now seemingly barbaric methods such as bloodletting, which at the time was said to remedy hundreds of diseases. Sometimes, people got better. But most of the time, they got worse. And doctors were never sure why.

By the nineteenth century, people began to blame disease on "miasmas" or "bad airs" that floated around dangerously. As hare-brained as it sounds today, "miasma theory" was actually an improvement over humorism because it spawned sanitary reforms that had the effect of removing real disease agents—bacteria. For example, in 1854, when cholera gripped London, the miasma explanation inspired massive, state-sponsored clearing of the air by draining cesspools. A physician of the time, John Snow, was able to isolate the pattern of new cholera cases and to conclude that new cases correlated to proximity to a specific water pump on Broad Street. Disease, he concluded, correlated with that pump—and therefore cholera was not transmitted through miasma, but likely through contaminated water. Snow's work saved countless lives—and he has subsequently been recognized as one of the most important physicians in history.

But while an improvement, Snow's analysis still didn't get to the *root cause* of what actually made those people sick.

Enter Louis Pasteur who, in the mid-1800s, conducted the critical experiments establishing that bacteria—or more simply, "germs"—were the cause of many common diseases. The wide-spread acceptance of Pasteur's work led quickly to the first vaccines and antibiotics, as well as a technique for making dairy products safe for consumption.

Why was Pasteur so successful, after hundreds of years of searching for explanations for the mysteries of human disease? Put simply, it was because Pasteur's work helped develop *a theory*— germ theory—that described the actual causal mechanisms of disease transfer. Before Pasteur, there were either crude and untestable guesses or statements of broad correlation without an underlying causal mechanism. Pasteur's work demonstrated that germs were transmitted through a process: microorganisms, too small to see with the naked eye, that live in the air, in water, on objects, and on skin. They can invade hosts (in this case, humans) and grow and reproduce within those hosts. Identifying the process by which people get sick allowed the development of ways to prevent its spread—in effect to interrupt that process, most notably through personal and social hygiene measures. We all owe Pasteur a debt of enormous gratitude, but his contribution was far greater than even the monumental direct descendants of his work—such as pasteurization and penicillin. He helped fundamentally change our understanding of biology and played a critical role in the rapid evolution of medicine from an art to a science, saving millions of lives in the process.

Shifting our understanding from educated guesses and correlation to an underlying causal mechanism is profound. Truly uncovering a causal mechanism changes everything about the way we solve problems—and, perhaps more important, prevents them. Take, for example, a more modern arena: automobile manufacturing.

When was the last time you got into your car and worried about whether it would start? The good news is that it's probably been longer than you can remember since that prospect crossed your mind. But as recently as the 1980s, that wasn't the case.

There were, certainly, plenty of decent cars coming out of

Detroit, but there were also a worrying number of lemons, cars that never quite seemed to work properly. No sooner had a technician repaired or replaced one component that had failed in a lemon, than another and then another seemed to follow suit. Multiple system failures conspired to make complete repair impossible. It was a frustrating situation for both manufacturers and buyers.

From one point of view, it's not surprising that lemons were common. A typical car contains nearly thirty thousand individual parts in all. Many of these are prebuilt—like the starter motor or the seats. Still, a typical auto manufacturing line will receive around two thousand unique parts from several hundred different suppliers, arriving from as many as seventeen different countries. The complexity of taking so many things from so many different sources and turning them into a working car is a miracle in itself. Indeed, for years the explanation for poor quality cars was that there is inherent randomness in manufacturing. You can't possibly get everything right, all the time. Much the same way companies think about innovation now.

Manufacturers soldiered on, trying to fix the problem as best as they could. They added extra inventory, inspectors, and rework stations to manage all the problems that the assembly line unfailingly generated. But with these fixes, unfortunately, costs and complexity ballooned. The processes they created simply mitigated the problems, but they were no closer to getting to the root cause of lemons. Instead, US car manufacturers had unwittingly designed a process that was *highly effective* at producing costly, inconsistent, and unreliable automobiles.

Amazingly, though, that's no longer the case. The Japanese auto manufacturers, inspired by the work of W. Edwards Deming and Joseph M. Juran, dramatically improved the quality of their automobiles in the 1970s and 80s.

The answer was found in theory. The Japanese experimented relentlessly to learn the *cause* of manufacturing defects. If they could only identify the root cause of each and every problem, they believed, then they could design a process to prevent that error from recurring. In this way, manufacturing errors were rarely repeated, quality improved continuously, and costs declined precipitously. In short, what the Japanese proved is that in spite of inherent complexity, it is possible to reliably and efficiently produce quality cars, when you focus on improving the manufacturing *process*. Japanese manufacturers didn't have the luxury of attempting to correct lemons after they rolled off the assembly line. If they were going to make any cars that an average Japanese consumer could afford to buy, Toyota and others would have to develop a process quite different from the prevailing mainstream: they would need to design defects *out* of the process.

When the Japanese encountered a defect, they treated it the way a scientist would treat an anomaly: an opportunity to understand what caused it; in this case to improve the manufacturing process. Defects turned out to have very specific causes and, once identified and understood, these causes could be corrected and the process altered or removed.

Toyota developed processes that ensured that every defect was identified and fixed as soon as it was created. As long as Toyota is continually identifying "anomalies" in the manufacturing process, every single defect is seen as an opportunity to make the process better. There are, in effect, a set of rules that ensure that this happens. For example, an employee must never add value to a part until it is ready to be used in the next step of adding value. It must be done in the same way, every time. That way managers know, definitely, that the value-adding step worked with the next step in the process. That creates an environment of repeated scientific experimentation. Each time it's done the same way constitutes a test of whether doing it that way, to those specifications, will result in perfection every time.

For Toyota, the theory was embodied in the set of processes

they developed to lead to defect-free manufacturing. Each activity can be seen as an individual if-then statement: "If we do *this*, then *that* will be the result." Through this theory of manufacturing, the quality movement was born. As a consequence, the Americans took what they'd learned from their Japanese competitors to heart and the US automobile industry today churns out very reliable cars.

Innovation, in a very real sense, exists in a "pre–quality revolution" state.[1] Managers accept flaws, missteps, and failure as an inevitable part of the process of innovation. They have become so accustomed to putting Band-Aids on their uneven innovation success that too often they give no real thought to what's causing it in the first place.

HOW TO THINK, NOT WHAT TO THINK

As an academic, I'm asked hundreds of times a year to offer opinions on specific business challenges in industries or organizations in which I have no special knowledge. Yet I'm able to provide insight because there is a toolbox full of theories that teach me not what to think but rather *how* to think. Good theory is the best way I know to frame problems in such a way that we ask the right questions to get us to the most useful answers. Embracing theory is not to mire ourselves in academic minutiae but, quite the opposite, to focus on the supremely practical question of *what causes what*.

Theory has a voice, but no agenda. A theory doesn't change its mind: it doesn't apply to some companies or people and not to others. Theories are not right or wrong. They provide accurate predictions, given the circumstances you are in.

In my MBA course, "Building and Sustaining a Successful Enterprise," we study theories regarding the various dimensions of the job of general managers. When the students understand these theories, we put them "on"—like a set of lenses—to examine a case about a company. We discuss what each of the theories can tell us about why problems and opportunities emerged for the company.

We then use the theories to predict what problems and opportunities are likely to occur in the future for that company, and we use the theories to predict what actions the managers will need to take to address them. I believe that good theory is essential for effective management practice and the most powerful tool I can offer my students.

Over the years, I've come to the conclusion that good theory is what has been missing in the discussions about how companies can create successful innovations. Is innovation truly a crapshoot? Or is innovation difficult because we don't know what causes it to succeed? I've watched so many smart, capable managers wrestle with all kinds of innovation challenges and nagging questions, but seldom the most fundamental one: *What causes a customer to purchase and use a particular product or service?*

We believe Jobs Theory, at last, provides an answer.

DEFINING THE JOB

There is a simple, but powerful, insight at the core of our theory: customers don't buy products or services; they pull them into their lives to make progress. We call this progress the "job" they are trying to get done, and in our metaphor we say that customers "hire" products or services to solve these jobs. When you understand that concept, the idea of uncovering consumer jobs makes intuitive sense. But as we have suggested, our definition of a Job to Be Done is precise—and we need to take a step back and unpack the elements to develop a complete theory of jobs.

Progress

We define a "job" as the *progress that a person is trying to make in a particular circumstance.* This definition of a job is not simply a new way of categorizing customers or their problems. It's key to understanding *why* they make the choices they make. The choice of the word "progress" is deliberate. It represents *movement* toward a goal or aspiration. A job is always a process to make progress, it's rarely a discrete event. A job is not necessarily just a "problem" that arises, though one form the progress can take is the resolution of a specific problem and the struggle it entails.

Circumstance

Second, the idea of a "circumstance" is intrinsic to the definition of a job. A job can only be defined—and a successful solution created—relative to the *specific context* in which it arises. There are dozens of questions that could be important to answer in defining the circumstance of a job. *"Where are you?" "When is it?" "Who are you with?" "While doing what?" "What were you doing half an hour ago?" "What will you be doing next?" "What social or cultural or political pressures exert influence?"* And so on. Our notion of a circumstance can extend to other contextual factors as well, such as life-stage (*"just out of college?" "stuck in a midlife crisis?" "nearing retirement?"*), family status (*"married, single, divorced?" "newborn baby, young children at home, adult parents to take care of?"*), or financial status (*"underwater in debt?" "ultra-high net worth?"*) just to name a few. The circumstance is fundamental to defining the job (and finding a solution for it), because the nature of the progress desired will always be strongly influenced by the circumstance.

The emphasis on the *circumstance* is not hair-splitting or simple semantics—it is fundamental to the Job to Be Done. In our experience, managers usually don't take this into account. Rather they typically follow one of four primary organizing principles in their innovation quest—or some composite thereof:

- Product attributes
- Customer characteristics
- Trends
- Competitive response

The point isn't that any of these categories are bad or wrong—and they're just a sampling of the most common. But they are insufficient, and therefore not predictive of customer behaviors.

Functional, Social, and Emotional Complexity

Finally, a job has an inherent complexity to it: it not only has functional dimensions, but it has *social* and *emotional* dimensions, too. In many innovations, the focus is often entirely on the functional or practical need. But in reality, consumers' social and emotional needs can far outweigh any functional desires. Think of how you would hire childcare. Yes, the functional dimensions of that job are important—will the solution safely take care of your children in a location and manner that works well in your life—but the social and emotional dimensions probably weigh more heavily on your choice. *"Who will I trust with my children?"*

WHAT IS A JOB?

To summarize, the key features of our definition are:

- A job is the progress that an individual seeks in a given circumstance.
- Successful innovations enable a customer's desired progress, resolve struggles, and fulfill unmet aspirations. They perform jobs that formerly had only inadequate or nonexistent solutions.
- Jobs are never simply about the functional—they have important social and emotional dimensions, which can be even more powerful than functional ones.
- Because jobs occur in the flow of daily life, the *circumstance* is central to their definition and becomes the essential unit of innovation work—not customer characteristics, product attributes, new technology, or trends.
- Jobs to Be Done are ongoing and recurring. They're seldom discrete "events."

WHAT ISN'T A JOB?

A well-defined job offers a kind of innovation blueprint. This is very different from the traditional marketing concept of "needs" because it entails a much higher degree of specificity about what you're solving for. Needs are ever present and that makes them necessarily more generic. *"I need to eat"* is a statement that is almost always true. *"I need to feel healthy." "I need to save for retirement."* Those needs are important to consumers, but their generality provides only the vaguest of direction to innovators as to how to satisfy them. Needs are analogous to trends—directionally useful, but totally insufficient for defining exactly what will cause a customer to choose one product or service over another. Simply needing to eat isn't going to cause me to pick one solution over another—or even pull any solution into my life at all. I might skip a meal. And needs, by themselves, don't explain all behavior: I might eat when I'm not hungry at all for a myriad of reasons.

Jobs take into account a far more complex picture. The *circumstances* in which I need to eat, and the other set of needs that might be critical to me at that moment, can vary wildly. Think back to our milk shake example. I may opt to hire a milk shake to resolve a job that arises in my own life. What will cause me to choose the milk shake are the bundle of needs that are in play *in those particular circumstances*. That bundle includes not only needs that are purely functional or practical (*"I'm hungry and I need something for breakfast"*), but also social and emotional (*"I'm alone on a long, boring commute and want to entertain myself, but I'd be embarrassed if one of my colleagues caught me with a milk shake in my hand so early in the morning"*). In those circumstances, some of my needs have a higher priority than others. I might, for example, opt to swing into the drive-through (where I won't be seen) of the fast-food chain for a milk shake for that morning commute. But under different circumstances—I have my son with me, it's dinnertime, and I want to feel like a good dad—the relative importance of each of my needs may cause me to hire the milk shake for an entirely different set of reasons. Or to turn to another solution to my job altogether.

Many wonderful inventions have been, unwittingly, built only around satisfying a very general "need." Take, for example, the Segway, a two-wheeled, self-balancing electric vehicle invented by Dean Kamen. In spite of the media frenzy around the release of Kamen's "top secret" invention that was supposed to change transportation forever, the Segway was, by most measures, a flop. It had been conceived around the need of more efficient personal transportation. But whose need? When? Why? In what circumstances? What else matters in the moment when somebody might be trying to get someplace more efficiently? The Segway was a cool invention, but it didn't solve a Job to Be Done that a lot of people shared. I see them from time to time in tourist spots around Boston or in our local mall, but especially compared with the prelaunch hype, very few people felt compelled to pull the Segway into their lives.

On the other end of the spectrum from needs are what I'll call the guiding principles of my life—overarching themes in my life that are ever present, just as needs are. I want to be a good husband, I want to be a valued member of my church, I want to inspire my students, and so on. These are critically important guiding principles to the choices I make in my life, but they're not my Jobs to Be Done. Helping me feel like a good dad is not a Job to Be Done. It's important to me, but it's not going to trigger me to pull one product over another into my life. The concept is too abstract. A company couldn't create a product or service to help me feel like a good dad without knowing the particular circumstances in which I'm trying to achieve that. The jobs I *am* hiring for are those that help me overcome the obstacles that get in the way of making progress toward the themes of my life—in specific circumstances. The full set of Jobs to Be Done as I go through life may roll up, collectively, into the major themes of my life, but they're not the same thing.

SEEING THE JOB?

Because of the inherent complexity of jobs, insights from observing customers in their moments of struggle do not easily break down into bits of data that can be fed into spreadsheets to be analyzed. In practice, seeing a job clearly and fully characterizing it can be tricky. Jobs insights are fragile—they're more like stories than statistics. When we deconstruct coherent customer episodes into binary bits, such as "male/female," "large company/small company," "new customer/existing customer," we destroy meaning in the process. Jobs Theory doesn't care whether a customer is between the ages of forty and forty-five and what flavor choice they made that day. Jobs Theory is not primarily focused on "who" did something, or "what" they did—but on "why." Understanding jobs is about *clustering* insights into a coherent picture, rather than segmenting down to finer and finer slices.

When I share Jobs Theory with people, they often find it to be both intuitive and revelatory. It just makes sense. They can easily think of jobs in their own lives and their misdirected efforts to satisfy them. But I also know that understanding it well enough to implement in practice can take some effort. It goes against the habits that so many managers have honed over years of practice.

One thought experiment we've found helpful to really grasp a job is to imagine you are filming a minidocumentary of a person struggling to make progress in a specific circumstance.

Your Video Should Capture Essential Elements:

I. **What progress is that person trying to achieve?** What are the functional, social, and emotional dimensions of the desired progress?

For example, a job that occurs in a lot of people's lives: *"I want to have a smile that will make a great first impression in my work and personal life"*; or a struggle many managers might relate to: *"I want the sales force I manage to be better equipped to succeed in their job so that the churn in staff goes down."*

2. **What are the circumstances of the struggle?** Who, when, where, while doing what?

   "I see a dentist twice a year and do all the right things to keep my teeth clean, but they never look white enough to me" or *"It seems like every week, another one of my guys is giving notice because he's burned out and I'm spending half my time recruiting and training new people."*

3. **What obstacles are getting in the way of the person making that progress?**

   For example, *"I've tried a couple of whitening toothpastes and they don't really work—they're just a rip-off"* or *"I've tried everything I can think of to motivate my sales staff: bonus programs for them, offsite bonding days, I've bought them a variety of training tools. And they still can't tell me what's going wrong."*

4. **Are consumers making do with imperfect solutions through some kind of compensating behavior?** Are they buying and using a product that imperfectly performs the job? Are they cobbling together a workaround solution involving multiple products? Are they doing nothing to solve their dilemma at all?

   For example, *"I've bought one of those expensive home whitening kits, but you have to wear this awful mouth guard overnight and it kind of burns my teeth . . ."* or *"I have to spend time making sales calls myself—and I don't have time for that!"*

5. **How would they define what "quality" means for a better solution, and what tradeoffs are they willing to make?**

   For example, *"I want the whitening performance of a professional dental treatment, without the cost and inconvenience"* or *"There are tons of 'products' and services I can purchase. But none of them actually help me do the job."*

These details are not arbitrary—they're rich in context and meaning—and answering these questions enables you to fully flesh out the complexity of the job. In this sense, Jobs Theory is an integration tool. When you identify a struggle to make progress, you can begin to infer not only the practical but the critical unseen or unspoken social and emotional dimensions of the Job to Be Done. Think of me standing in that fast-food chain with my son in the afternoon. That's a completely different video from one of me pulling in to the restaurant to grab a morning milk shake.

Consider some of the most recent entrepreneurial success stories through the lens of a Job to Be Done. Take Airbnb, for example. Airbnb could be reduced to its function—providing a place to stay when traveling. On that level, it's competing against hotels. And by traditional measures of quality in the hotel industry, Airbnb is a far inferior option. Who would pay to stay on an air mattress on the floor of a stranger's apartment—or sleep in a stranger's spare bed—rather than stay in the privacy of their own hotel room?

It turns out, lots of people.

People weren't hiring Airbnb only because it's a place to stay. They were hiring Airbnb because having a place to stay allows them to be someplace so they can participate in something in which they want to be part—and because it offers a more authentic local experience than a cookie-cutter, one-size-fits-the-world hotel chain.

Airbnb initially identified a Job to Be Done in cofounder Brian Chesky's own life. As a new college graduate in San Francisco, Chesky could barely afford his own rent, let alone find the fees to attend a local design conference. When he realized that all the hotels in the area were sold out—and that there must be other aspiring designers with the same struggle he had—he came up with the idea to "rent" three air mattresses in his apartment to help fund his own conference attendance. He could imagine himself as one of those air mattress renters if he found himself in the same circumstances in another city. He might desperately want to participate in something, but he didn't want to feel like a tourist or rack up credit card debt to make it happen.

Just because Airbnb didn't stack up well compared with hotels or motels by traditional measures didn't mean there wasn't a very real struggle for progress for which Airbnb was a better option. The circumstances in which consumers would hire Airbnb are very different from those in which they'd hire a hotel.[2] Airbnb isn't just competing with hotels, it's competing with staying with friends. Or not making the trip at all.

On the surface, it was an improbable success story: "At the beginning people said, 'You're out of your mind for starting this company. Nobody's going to use it. Only crazy people are going to rent a room in someone's apartment,'" recalls LinkedIn founder and Airbnb investor Reid Hoffman. "But sometimes," Hofmann says now, "it's a job you can't currently see."

Throughout this book we will refer to jobs in shorthand, simplistic terms for ease of reference—but it's important to emphasize that a well-defined job is multilayered and complex. And that is actually a good thing. Why? Because it means that perfectly satisfying someone's job likely requires not just creating a product, but engineering and delivering a whole set of experiences that address the many dimensions of the job and then integrating those experiences into the company's processes (as we'll discuss in depth later in the book). When you've done that well, it's almost impossible for competitors to copy.

SHIFTING COMPETITIVE LANDSCAPE

It's important to note that we don't "create" jobs, we discover them. Jobs themselves are enduring and persistent, but the way we solve them can change dramatically over time. Think, for example, of the job of sharing information across long distances. That underlying job has not changed, but our solutions for it have: from Pony Express to telegraph to air mail to email and so on. For example, teenagers have had the job of communicating with each other without the nosy intervention of parents for centuries. Years ago, they passed notes in the school hallway or pulled the telephone cord all the way into the furthest corner of their room. But in recent years, teens have started hiring Snapchat, a smartphone app that allows messages to be delivered and then disappear almost instantly and a whole host of other things that could not even have been imagined a few decades ago. The creators of Snapchat understood the job well enough to create a superior solution. But that doesn't mean Snapchat isn't vulnerable to other competitors coming along with a better understanding of the complex set of social, emotional, and functional needs of teenagers *in particular circumstances*. Our understanding of the Job to Be Done can always get better. Adopting new technologies can improve the way we solve Jobs to Be Done. But what's important is that you focus on understanding the underlying job, not falling in love with your solution for it.

For innovators, understanding the job is to understand what consumers care most about in that moment of trying to make progress. Jobs Theory enables innovators to make the myriad, detailed tradeoffs in terms of which benefits are essential and which are extraneous to a new offering. Understanding the *circumstance-specific* hiring criteria triggers a whole series of important insights, perhaps most notably that the competitive field is likely completely different from what you might have imagined.

Here's one example to illustrate the point. When a smoker takes a cigarette break, on one level he's simply seeking the nicotine his body craves. That's the functional dimension. But that's not all that's going on. He's hiring cigarettes for the emotional benefit of calming him down, relaxing him. And if he works in a typical office building, he's forced to go outside to a designated smoking area. But that choice is social, too—he can take a break from work and hang around with his buddies. From this perspective, people hire Facebook for many of the same reasons. They log onto Facebook during the middle of the workday to take a break from work, relax for a few minutes while thinking about other things, and convene around a virtual water cooler with far-flung friends. In some ways, Facebook is actually competing with cigarettes to be hired for the same Job to Be Done. Which the smoker chooses will depend on the circumstances of his struggle in that particular moment.

Managers and industry analysts like to keep their framing of competition simple—put like companies, industries, and products in the same buckets. Coke versus Pepsi. Sony PlayStation versus Xbox. Butter versus margarine. This conventional view of the competitive landscape puts tight constraints around what innovation is relevant and possible, as it emphasizes benchmarking and keeping up with the Joneses. Through this lens, opportunities to grab market share can seem finite, with most companies settling for gaining a few percentage points, within a zero-sum game.

But from a Jobs Theory perspective, the competition is seldom limited to products that the market chooses to lump into the same category. Netflix CEO Reed Hastings made this clear when recently asked by legendary venture capitalist John Doerr if Netflix was competing with Amazon. "Really we compete with everything you do to relax," he told Doerr. "We compete with video games. We compete with drinking a bottle of wine. That's a particularly tough one! We compete with other video networks. Playing board games."

The competitive landscape shifts to something new, maybe uncomfortably new, but one with fresh potential when you see competition through a Jobs to Be Done lens.

For example, BMW had long described itself as being in the business of "high performance cars," going so far at one point as to unabashedly advertise it as a "man's car." But with the auto industry in a nosedive at the start of the 2008 recession, BMW's leadership team took a step back to assess what jobs consumers were hiring cars to do. What they found changed the company's entire view of the competitive landscape. With demand for green fuel-efficient cars becoming a top priority (California had just passed legislation that effectively banned combustion engines in the near future, for example), a trend toward urbanization, and fewer young people bothering to get their driver's license at all, BMW realized the real job was *mobility*. Get me painlessly from point A to point B. Yes, BMW was competing with traditional luxury cars, but it was also competing with Tesla, Uber, and Zipcar, and Google's self-driving (and Apple's reported) electric car projects. "We realized we were competing with companies whose names we couldn't pronounce eighteen months ago," recalls Steven Althaus, global director of brand management and marketing services at BMW. "We needed to start benchmarking outside of our category."

That led not only to the launch of the electric and hybrid BMWi line, but also to BMW's DriveNow, a pilot Zipcar-type sharing program that's been launched in Berlin, Vienna, San Francisco, and London. "We've changed from a supply side perspective to a demand side perspective," Althaus says—in effect, shifting from selling products to responding to jobs. That framing itself was a sea change for an auto manufacturer used to seeing its dealers as its primary customers. With that one leap, who the "customers" are and what they care about changes dramatically—as did BMW's perspective on innovation.

And BMW is not alone. The race is clearly on to determine who best understands consumers' Jobs to Be Done. Ford CEO Mark Fields spent much of late 2015 telling people that "we are not only thinking of ourselves as an automotive company, but also as a mobility company." General Motors (GM) invested in an alternative car service, Lyft, and then announced the launch of its own ride-sharing service, Maven, in early 2016. As part of the investment in Lyft, GM will work on developing an on-demand network of self-driving cars, an area of research to which Google, Tesla, and Uber have all begun to devote enormous resources.

Think of the path ahead through the lens of Jobs Theory.[3] Each company will have to understand the Job to Be Done in all its rich complexity. Then they'll have to consider and shape their offerings around the experiences that consumers will seek in solving their jobs—and help them surmount any roadblocks that get in their way of making progress. Competitive advantage will be granted to whoever understands and best solves the job.

What each of those companies makes of that new perspective will determine how successful their new efforts will be in the long run. Because if you don't know what you're really competing with, how could you ever hope to create something that consumers will choose to hire over all other potential solutions?

THE LIMITS OF JOBS THEORY

That's not to say that Jobs Theory is the answer for every question. The nature of the problem at hand will dictate if it's the best theory to understand what's causing what. That's true of every theory.

Sound theory—the kind that truly explains, predictably, what will cause what to happen—does not develop overnight. It has to be shaped, tested, and refined, and the context in which it does and does not apply must be understood. But even if a theory doesn't apply to some particular application, it's still valuable because knowing when a particular theory doesn't help explain something will allow you to turn to others to find better answers. That's a hallmark of good theory. It dispenses its advice in if-then statements.

Consider man's early attempt at flight. Early researchers observed strong correlation between feathers and wings and flight. As a result, their initial attempts at flight involved replicating what they believed allowed birds to soar. It was not until the Swiss-Dutch mathematician Daniel Bernoulli outlined what was to become known as Bernoulli's principle that we understood the importance of lift—the idea that when air flows across a shape we call an airfoil, the air underneath it pushes the airfoil up. Bird wings function as airfoils, and thus air flowing past their wings propels them upward. This same insight has resulted in the modern airfoils we see as airplane wings.

But even after the insight that lift, not wings and feathers, caused flight, scientists still had to hone the causal lens through trial-and-error experimentation in order to design successful aircraft. When an airplane crashed, researchers would then ask, "Was the design of the aircraft, or the materials used, at fault? Or was there something about the situation the pilot found herself in—a situation that demanded a different set of rules and techniques in order to avoid a crash?" Today the causal lenses in aviation are so advanced that engineers and pilots can not only guarantee flight, they can define precisely what rules the pilots need to follow in order to succeed in just about every possible circumstance—if the weather is bad, if the air pressure is high or low, and so on. The circumstances matter.

With all theory building, you have to be open to finding things that the theory can't explain—anomalies—and use them as an opportunity to strengthen it. We know, for example, that Jobs Theory is not useful if there is no real struggle for a consumer or the existing solutions are good enough. It's not useful when the decision to be made relies almost entirely on a mathematical analysis, such as commodities trading. Cost or efficiency is not a core element of a job. In those circumstances, there is not a complex bundle of social, emotional, and functional needs in search of progress. There are rational decisions to be made—and ones that can just as easily be made by a computer.

A theory is essentially a proposition: we propose this set of processes will help develop innovations that will be successful. But if someone has a better set of processes to deliver more consistently successful innovations, we welcome that in our quest to better refine this theory.

But until then, we believe Jobs Theory will make an enormous difference in the quest to shift innovation from a game of chance to a predictable endeavor. Opportunities, competitors, and what matters most to your customers may look very different, but they will also be very clear. Your perspective will be irrevocably shifted—but for the better.

A COPERNICAN REVOLUTION

For nearly eighteen centuries, Aristotle dominated scientific thinking. His observations and theories about our universe were so widely accepted that they were later deemed by the most powerful institution in the medieval Western world—the Catholic Church—to be the definitive truth. Among his many important insights: all "heavenly bodies" moved in perfect circles around the earth. Therefore, we could predict how the other planets would move, over time, by observing their progress along Aristotle's circles, with the earth at the center of it all. Aristotle was such a profoundly influential thinker and philosopher that his work stood almost completely unchallenged for centuries.

Except there was one problem. When ancient astronomers tried to chart and predict the progress of the planets around the earth, it didn't quite work. So they created a rather tortuous explanation. Planets did revolve in circles around the earth, but within those circles the planets also moved in what Ptolemy called "epicycles"—minirotations within the circles. With a complex pattern of circles within circles, it was possible to still predict the planets' movement around the earth. Except even the most precise calculations, taking complicated combinations of epicycles into account, could still only predict the movements within a margin of error. The best models were still off by as much as eight minutes of arc—about one and a third degree off a perfect 360°. Close enough for most people to call it accurate. But not, as it turns out, actually right.

Because Aristotle's was the accepted lens on the universe, centuries of medieval scientists and thinkers went to great lengths to make epicycles work. It wasn't until the sixteenth century, with one simple but profound observation, that Renaissance astronomer Nicolaus Copernicus reframed our view of the universe. The planets revolved not around the earth, but around the sun. Finally, understanding that provided a foundation for some of the most important advances in history and the foundation for modern astronomy and calculus.

Of course, it took eighteen centuries for someone like Copernicus to see and articulate the flaws in Aristotle's logic. And even he died without knowing that the world would accept he was right. Changing a well-established view of the world rarely happens overnight—and even when it happens, it still takes time to refine and perfect the right new perspective.

In the world of innovation, many companies are stuck in a world of creating "epicycles": elaborate approximations, estimations, and extrapolations. Because we gather, fine-tune, and cross-reference all manner of data, it seems like we should be getting better and better at predicting success. But if we fail to understand *why* customers make the choices they make, we're just getting better and better at a fundamentally flawed process. Without the right understanding of the *causal mechanism* at the center of the innovation universe, companies are trying to make sense of the universe revolving around the earth. They're forced to rely on an array of borrowed best practices, probabilistic tools, and tips and tricks that have worked for other companies, but which can't guarantee success. As you look at innovation through the lenses of the Jobs Theory, what you see is not the *customer* at the center of the innovation universe, but the customer's *Job to Be Done*. It may seem like a small distinction—just a few minutes of arc—but it matters a great deal. In fact, it changes everything.

- While many in the business world associate the word "theory" with something purely academic or abstract, nothing could be further from the truth. Theories that explain causality are among the most important and practical tools business leaders can have.

- The field of innovation is in need of better theory, especially for the foundational question "What causes a customer to purchase and use a particular product or service?"

- Jobs Theory answers this question by asserting that customers purchase and use (or "hire" in our jobs metaphor) products and services to satisfy jobs that arise in their lives. A job is defined as *the progress that a customer desires to make in a particular circumstance.*

- This definition is specific and important: Fully understanding a customer's job requires understanding the progress a customer is trying to make *in particular circumstances* and understanding all of its functional, social, and emotional dimensions—as well as the tradeoffs the customer is willing to make.

- Once you understand the customer's Job to Be Done, it brings into sharp relief the true competition you face to be hired. This provides critical information for how to innovate to make your solution more attractive than any competitor's.

- Do you understand the real reason *why* your customers choose your products or services? Or why they choose something else instead?

- How do your products or services help your customers to make progress in their lives? In which circumstances are they trying to make that progress? What are the functional, emotional, and social dimensions of this progress?

- What is competing with your products and services to address these jobs? Are there competitors outside of those included in the traditional view of your industry?

NOTES

1. Some meaningful progress has been made in understanding what it takes to systematize innovation in large organizations. My co-author David Duncan and his colleague Scott Anthony, managing partner at Innosight, have described in detail the foundational components and operations of any well-functioning innovation system, what they refer to as a "Growth Factory." Their work has guided the efforts of some of the most successful Fortune 100 companies as they've built their global innovation capabilities. Other writers have also contributed to our understanding of how to systematize innovation, most notably Vijay Govindarajan at the Tuck School of Business. The Theory of Jobs, however, is focused on a different question: "What causes a customer to purchase and use a particular product or service?" It's critical to have a theory to answer this question to ensure that the innovation system you establish is pointed in the right direction and works on innovations that have the best chance of success. Anthony, Scott D., and David S. Duncan. *Building a Growth Factory*. Boston: Harvard Business Review Press, 2012.

2. This was the case for Airbnb in the early years. In recent years, Airbnb has identified other jobs at the higher end of the market—and is successfully competing there, too.

3. There's a tool, called "discovery-driven planning," that can help companies test whether their strategy to respond to the job they've identified will be fruitful before they sink too many resources into any one path. It forces them to articulate what assumptions need to be proved true in order for the strategy to succeed. The academics who created this process, Ian MacMillan and Rita McGrath, called it discovery-driven planning, but it might be easier to think about it as "What has to prove true for this to work?" Companies seldom think about whether to pursue new opportunities by asking this question. Instead, they often unintentionally stack the deck for failure from

the beginning. They make decisions to go ahead with an investment based on what initial projections suggest will happen, but then they never actually test whether those initial projections are accurate. So, they often find themselves far down the road, adjusting projections and assumptions to fit what is actually happening rather than testing and making thoughtful choices before they get too far in.

In almost every case of a project failing, mistakes were made in one or more of the critical assumptions upon which the projections and decisions were based. But the company didn't realize that until they were too far down the road. Money, time, and energy had already been assigned to the project; the company is 100 percent committed; and the team is now on the line to make it work. Nobody wants to go back to management and say, "You know those assumptions we made? Turns out they weren't so accurate after all. . . ." Projects end up getting approved on the basis of incorrect guesses, as opposed to which project is actually most likely to work out.

CHAPTER 3

Jobs in the Wild

THE BIG IDEA

Jobs Theory is not just another framework or marketing approach, but a powerful lens that has driven breakthrough innovation and transformational growth in some of the world's most successful organizations—in wildly diverse arenas. Jobs Theory transforms how you define the business you're in, the size and shape of the market in which you compete, and who your competitors are. This enables you to see customers where there were none, ideas for solutions where there were only problems, and opportunity where you least expect it. Here's how.

Standing in front of the graduating class of Southern New Hampshire University (SNHU) in 2015, President Paul LeBlanc decided to go off script. It was the third commencement ceremony that day—the total number of graduating students and families was too large to fit into the auditorium in one sitting, even in the twelve thousand seats of Verizon Wireless Arena, so the school had to stage three separate events. Instead of wading into the usual jokes and graduation platitudes, a wide smile spread across LeBlanc's face as he turned his focus to those in caps and gowns before him. "If you served in the military or are serving in the military, and are graduating today, please stand for a moment," he asked. About half of those in caps and gowns stood. "If you are, as I am, the first generation in your family to get an undergraduate degree, stand." Roughly half of the crowd got to their feet. "If you're getting a degree today, and you also have kids, please stand." By then, virtually every member of the graduating class had been on his or her feet. Usually a poised and polished speaker, LeBlanc choked up for a moment as the crowd roared. Achieving that degree, against considerable odds, was an enormous accomplishment for the people in caps and gowns that day. "They recognized what they'd done," LeBlanc later recalled. "No one in that graduation ceremony had it handed to them. There's so much that gets in the way of that happening—finances, busy lives, lack of academic preparedness, feeling like you don't belong. They'd truly earned that moment."

The people in the auditorium that day were just the tip of the iceberg. In fact, the vast majority of SNHU's students will never set foot on its modest Manchester, New Hampshire, campus. But that hasn't stopped those students from making progress toward their goals. In fact, so many have chosen SNHU that by the end of fiscal 2016, SNHU was closing in on $535 million in revenues—a 34 percent compounded annual growth rate for the past six years. Routinely lauded by *U.S. News & World Report* (and other publications) as one of the most innovative colleges in America, the school also has the distinction of being ranked one of the best places to work by the *Chronicle of Higher Education*. In 2012, *Fast Company* magazine named SNHU as one of the most innovative organizations *in the world*—ahead of LinkedIn, Starbucks, and the National Football League.

A decade before, none of that might have seemed possible—to either the students or LeBlanc. In 2003, when LeBlanc first became president of SNHU,[1] the seventy-year-old college was a relatively unknown second-tier institution. Originally founded as an accounting and secretarial school, it had become a mishmash of specialties—culinary arts, business, and justice programs—with just a few thousand students.

All around the country, similar colleges were facing deep financial troubles, closing or merging just to stay alive. The onset of the recession five years later made things look even worse. Enrollment began to fall and budget pressures just to tread water were overwhelming.

Around that same time, LeBlanc attended a working group at Harvard Business School that I put on every year to help market-leading companies avoid their own innovator's dilemma. Over the course of the day, we discussed the milk shake story and the Theory of Jobs to Be Done, which immediately resonated with LeBlanc.

Like most higher educational institutions, SNHU essentially treated all students the same. The university's longtime bread-and-butter strategy had relied on appealing to a traditional student body: eighteen-year-olds, fresh out of high school, continuing on a traditional educational path. In essence, "Come to this picturesque New Hampshire campus and you'll get a solid education for a reasonable price." The marketing and outreach were generic for everyone, regardless of their circumstances, and the policies and delivery models that served the school were designed to appeal to a "typical" student that really didn't exist. This one-size-fits-all perspective was reminiscent of the milk shake dilemma—only in this case they were trying to design a one-size-fits-all education for the "average" student.

What job were students actually hiring SNHU to do? Simply asking themselves that question, LeBlanc says, led them to an important insight. Not only was there one answer to that question—there were two.

Almost nothing had changed in SNHU's approach to recruiting

high school graduates in decades. It relied on traditional marketing and word of mouth to get prospects to the campus, where SNHU would wax poetic about the academics or financial aid or future career prospects. But through a jobs lens, LeBlanc says, the school realized that when these prospective students toured the campus, there were actually very few questions about these subjects. *Parents* of those students might ask those questions, but the students themselves focused on something entirely different. The students' questions centered on the experiences they hoped to have in college—experiences they'd been anticipating for years. *"Do you have a sports team I can root for? Do you have climbing walls? Will I have lots of interaction with full-time faculty with whom I can have long conversations about the meaning of life?"* The prospective students—in the circumstance of graduating from high school and being away from home for the first time—were not focused on the *functional dimensions* of their education; they were hiring SNHU for the coming-of-age experience. And SNHU had plenty of competitors for the roughly three thousand coming-of-age students it expected to enroll each year. There are a handful of established local colleges, such as the University of New Hampshire or Franklin Pierce University, that compete every year for more or less the same pool of applicants. In that competition, SNHU knew exactly how it would typically fare—win some, lose some, draw others. That ratio had not moved in years. It was hard to see much potential for growth.

By contrast, however, SNHU had an online academic program, known as distance learning. It was "a sleepy operation on a nondescript corner of the main campus," as LeBlanc describes it, but it had been able to attract a steady stream of students who wanted to resume an aborted education at a later stage of their lives. The online program had been launched a decade before, but it was treated as a side project, and the university put almost no resources into it.

On paper, all the students might have looked similar, rolling up into one category based on where they were in terms of course completion. A thirty-five-year-old working toward an accounting degree needs the same courses as an eighteen-year-old working toward the same degree, right? Don't they both need quality education at affordable prices?

COMPETING WITH NOTHING

But with the lens of Jobs to Be Done, LeBlanc and his team saw that the job these nontraditional students were hiring SNHU to do had almost nothing in common with the job coming-of-age undergraduates were hiring it for, and that it was framed by a very different circumstance. The average online student is thirty years old and juggling work and family while trying to squeeze in an education. Many of them have some college credits, but stopped their education along the way for a myriad of reasons. Often they were still carrying debt from that unfinished experience. But life has told them it's time to go back to school; they realize they need further academic credentials to improve their career prospects and thus to improve their family's lives. They've already had all the coming-of-age experiences they can handle. They need higher education to provide just four things: convenience, customer service, credentials, and speedy completion times. This, LeBlanc's team realized, was an enormous opportunity.

SNHU's online program wasn't in competition with the same set of local competitors at all. It was competing with other national online programs, including both traditional colleges and some of the for-profit specialty programs, such as Kaplan, University of Phoenix, ITT Technical Institute, and more—created and designed to provide students with training and credentials that might help them get a better job. But even more significantly, SNHU was also competing with *nothing*: nonconsumption. People choosing to do nothing to further their education at that stage of life. With that perspective, the size of the market suddenly went from seeming finite and hardly worth fighting for, to one with enormous untapped potential. Who wouldn't want to be competing with *nothing*?

But LeBlanc and his team quickly realized that very little about SNHU's existing policies, structures, and procedures were set up to support the actual job of online learners. The division had managed to bring in a respectable $32 million in revenues, but it was almost a miracle that so many students had found SNHU in the first place—and stuck it out to reach graduation.

Take, for example, the way that SNHU (and many other universities) typically discussed financial aid with prospective students. For a typical high school student, a conversation began sometime in their junior year, during which time SNHU would provide some basic information about financial aid. Neither student nor university expected to have to offer any more specifics for at least a year, after formal application and financial disclosure by the student's parents—when a college admissions offer was made. The financial-aid process at SNHU was structured around the ability to have a leisurely, low-level-of-urgency conversation with prospective students. Even responding to a query could reasonably be expected to take weeks.

If a prospective student made a query through SNHU's website, he'd receive a boilerplate response within twenty-four hours: "Dear Clayton, thank you for your interest. . . ." Then a week or so later, a packet of information—the same for everyone who inquired—would arrive in the mail. Then SNHU, like many universities, would simply wait for the prospective student to call or follow up in some way. And for many undergraduate candidates, particularly for the coming-of-age segment, that system worked fine. Because as they realized, the decision about financial aid might be important to their parents, but it wasn't critical to what the *students themselves* were hiring the university to do for them.

By contrast, financial considerations were enormously important for adult online learners. The job they were hiring a university to do was to provide them with credentials that would improve their professional prospects as quickly and efficiently as possible. When the leaders of SNHU thought about these students, it became clear how flawed the school's generic response to all prospects was. When an adult learner was actively online seeking information about a continuing education program, he or she was ripe, right then, to make a decision about what to do next. He'd probably thought about getting additional educational qualifications for a long time and, for him, starting the inquiry process was very close to the moment of making a decision. SNHU knew that its students were often moms and dads sitting at their laptop late at night after the kids have gone to bed, squeezing in the time to hunt and gather information in the first place. There was no leisurely response and follow-up that would meet their needs in those circumstances. For SNHU to wait twenty-four hours to send a generic response and then weeks later to provide candidates with any specific information about their own financial aid options was tantamount to not responding at all. What online learners required was completely different from what traditional students out of high school required, yet SNHU had been providing a single "average" solution for all.

For LeBlanc and his team, it was an "aha!" moment. The key was *finally asking the right question* that led them to better answers.

"We were frustrated and struggling with our inability to grow," he says now, "and focusing on the Jobs to Be Done felt like a no-brainer."

What had to change at SNHU as a consequence? "Pretty much everything," LeBlanc recalls, and on two different tracks corresponding to the two distinct jobs.

Instead of the second-class-citizen status the online portion of the university had been given since its inception, LeBlanc and his leadership team made it their focus. They moved the small online recruitment and administration team two miles away to new offices in a former mill yard in Manchester—a classic "disruptor" positioning that allowed the online team to grow unfettered by the physical and structural limitations of the traditional university policies and procedures. Then LeBlanc and his team led a session of about twenty of the top online faculty and administrators and charted out the entire admissions process—from first inquiry to first class—on a whiteboard. "It looked like a schematic from a nuclear submarine!" he says. The team circled all the hurdles that SNHU was throwing up—or not helping to overcome—in that process, with an eye toward the unique job of online learners, their unique circumstances, and the functional, social, and emotional dimensions of the job that were important to them. And then, one by one, they eliminated those hurdles and replaced them with experiences that would perfectly satisfy this job. There were literally dozens and dozens of decisions that came out of this new jobs focus, but to highlight a few, through the lens of the job:

1. **What are the experiences customers seek in order to make progress?** *There were no more leisurely responses to inquiries about financial aid.* That twenty-four-hours-later generic email was transformed into a follow-up phone call from someone at SNHU *in under ten minutes* of an inquiry. In the competitive online-learning world, the first online-learning institution to actually speak to a prospective student is most likely the one to close the sale. So instead of being a perfunctory follow-up, the phone call itself, LeBlanc says, was seen as a crucial opportunity to remove barriers for the prospective student. "You can uncover and surface a lot of anxiety issues," he says, "so those calls are with a well-trained counselor with all the information he needs at his fingertips [to help the student overcome whatever obstacles they're facing]. Calls can go on for an hour, an hour and a half.

At the end of the call, you're engaged with us. And we know you're much more likely to enroll."

2. **What obstacles must be removed?** *Decisions about a prospect's financial aid package and how much previous college courses would be counted toward an SNHU degree were resolved within days—* instead of weeks or even months.

3. **What are the social, emotional, and functional dimensions?** *The university's ads for the online program were completely re-oriented so that they focused on how it could fulfill the job for later-life learners.* The ads were aimed to resonate not just with the functional dimensions of the job, such as getting the training needed to advance in a career, but also with the emotional and social dimensions as well, such as the pride one feels in realizing a goal or the fulfillment of a commitment to a loved one. One ad featured a large SNHU bus roaming the country handing out large, traditionally framed diplomas to online learners who couldn't be on campus for graduation. "Who did you get this degree for?" the voice-over asks, as the commercial captures glowing graduates in their home environment. "I got it for me," one woman says, hugging her diploma. "I did this for my mom," beams a thirty-something man. "I did it for you, bud," one father says, holding back tears, as his young son chirps, "Congratulations, Daddy!"

But perhaps most important, SNHU realized that enrolling prospects in a first class was only the beginning of doing the job for them. To truly fulfill the job that those applicants were hiring continuing education to do for them, SNHU had to make sure it succeeded in meeting their own goals. SNHU sets up each new online student with a personal adviser, who stays in constant contact—and notices red flags even before the students might—in order to help them continue to make the progress they want to make. Haven't checked out this week's assignment by Wednesday or Thursday? Your adviser will check in with you. The unit test went badly? You can count on a call from your adviser to see not only what's going on with the class, but also what's going on in your life. Your laptop is causing you problems? An adviser might just send you a new one.

SNHU's staggering growth suggests that LeBlanc and his colleagues deeply understand these students' Jobs to Be Done. There are now twelve hundred College of Online and Continuing Education (COCE) staffers at that site in the former mill yard in Manchester, and more than seventy-five thousand students in thirty-six states and countries around the world. "There have been times when we almost broke the machine, we were outgrowing our systems so much," LeBlanc recalls. When growth has been that rapid, SNHU has dialed back its recruiting efforts until it can reinforce its internal support and systems. LeBlanc knows that if SNHU fails to deliver on the job, students will not hesitate to fire it and seek something that does the job better.

SNHU now routinely generates very healthy 10 percent surpluses, which in turn has allowed it to make major investments in infrastructure, provide award-winning working conditions for its employees, and keep tuition low for students (indeed, online students have had no tuition increases in the last four years). It has also allowed investment in continued cutting-edge innovations, such as SNHU's $2,500-a-year competency-based program, in which students can earn a degree based on demonstrating competency in various subjects, rather than hours logged in classes or fulfilling the right number of requisite courses. In a speech in 2013 at the University of Buffalo, President Barack Obama made a point of singling out SNHU for creating programs that allow students affordable options for pursuing advanced degrees.

Would LeBlanc and his team have stumbled onto a better way to grow online without asking the Jobs to Be Done questions? LeBlanc doesn't think so. "It gave us the language to start talking about it in our leadership team and more broadly on campus," he says. "It was a heuristic that was really useful for looking at what we had to do."

DEPTH *AND* BREADTH OF APPLICATION

Over the past decade, we've worked closely with many companies that provide helpful illustrations of how the Theory of Jobs to Be Done has helped transform innovation. Because Jobs Theory uncovers the cause of why consumers make the choices they do, it's useful in a wide range of industries and organizations—from the simplest consumer packaged goods to complex business-to-business solutions. In every case, uncovering why customers make choices allows organizations to better create solutions that get hired. We've chosen to highlight just a few here—and then later, throughout the book—to make clear the breadth of applicability of Jobs to Be Done.

For example, nothing sounds less innovative than a cheese company rolling out yet another type of cheese. But Sargento cleared $50 million in its first year with its prepackaged ultrathin slices, driving enormous category growth and exceeding $150 million in year two. Why did this product thrive, when the vast majority of the other thirty-four hundred consumer packaged goods launched in the same year didn't even survive their first twelve months in the market? Sargento's ultrathin sliced cheese was solving a job consumers were struggling with: *"How can I enjoy all of the delicious cheese experience that I love on my daily sandwich without the calories, fat, and guilt that come with it?"* Jobs Theory, explains Rod Hogan, vice president of New Business Development at Sargento, "forces you to define the offering in the context of a very specific consumer struggle. And that is neither easy nor natural for most large companies."

In its 2012–2016 annual Breakthrough Innovation Reports, Nielsen tracked over twenty thousand new product launches and identified just ninety-two that sold more than $50 million in year one and sustained sales in year two (excluding close-in line extensions). On the surface the list of breakthrough winners might seem random—International Delight Iced Coffee, Hershey's Reese's Minis, and Tidy Cats Lightweight, to name just a few—but they have one thing in common: Every single one of them nailed a poorly performed Job to Be Done.

JOBS IN A B2B WORLD

At the other end of the complexity spectrum is FranklinCovey. Formed in the 1997 merger between Franklin Quest and Covey Leadership Center (the latter was founded by Stephen R. Covey, the famed author of *7 Habits of Highly Effective People*)—the company had been struggling to gain a foothold for years. Revenue hit a peak of $589 million in 2000, but by 2009—after sales of businesses (including its iconic Franklin Planner and other planner-related business), streamlining, layoffs, and refocusing, it was down to $130 million. The company had survived some tough years—but was now intent on accelerating its growth.

Over the course of three years, Bob Whitman, the company's former chairman of the board who had assumed the role of CEO, personally visited nearly four hundred existing and potential customers for the company's line of B2B training offerings. On his eighth customer visit, something clicked. He was meeting with the chief learning officer of a Fortune 500 company that had used FranklinCovey content to train thirty-five hundred of its staff in improving personal and professional effectiveness. But this company had thirty-five *thousand* employees who should also have been potential beneficiaries of the training offerings FranklinCovey sold. "How come only thirty-five hundred people have been trained so far?" Whitman asked. The chief learning officer explained that he bought FranklinCovey training materials to help build a mindset and capabilities that were critical to the company's culture. But there were a lot of products that could help him do that.

HR professionals needed an array of offerings—such as Myers-Briggs testing and analysis, training in conflict resolution, delegation, navigating difficult conversations, project management, and so on, to roll out within the organization. FranklinCovey's offerings at the time were just one of many that HR personnel could tap. And as FranklinCovey had learned the hard way, learning-and-development budgets get cut when times get tough. There wasn't an infinite upside for FranklinCovey in creating more, new, and different products that more or less did the same thing as all the other options already available on the market.

But Whitman probed further: what was the chief learning officer really hiring FranklinCovey—and other—products to do? Using a jobs frame for the discussion, Whitman says, they uncovered a far more complex picture—one that clearly pointed to an unfulfilled job. Though the chief learning officer's team loved FranklinCovey products for learning and development, it hadn't been clear to their own internal customers—leaders inside the company—how these products helped them with the priorities they cared most about: driving customer loyalty and delivering growth.

As Whitman continued his visits to customers, he realized he was hearing the same thing over and over: for the people *buying* FranklinCovey products, their single biggest challenge was getting line leaders and other influencers within the company to recognize what they did in learning and development was mission critical. They wanted to be seen as vital, contributing members to the company's long-term goals. But they hadn't always been able to connect the work they were doing to something that business leaders would recognize as helping them achieve their objectives. These HR and learning professionals wanted their work to matter—*and to be acknowledged to matter*—in implementing their companies' most important priorities.

That insight led to years of reworking, rethinking, and repositioning all of FranklinCovey's offerings around its customers' key Jobs to Be Done. "It's been a fundamental part of how we think about everything," Whitman says. Historically, FranklinCovey would sell courses, typically to the chief human resources or learning officer. The FranklinCovey sales team would focus on identifying and selling the specific courses that a customer might need in any given year. But there was a flaw with that approach. If a CEO declared a set of priorities and goals that didn't match those particular courses, they weren't going to be hired. So FranklinCovey revised its approach: instead of selling courses, it now sells subscriptions that provide customers with nearly unlimited access to all its courses and content. Moreover, this content can be formulated into courses, bite-size learning modules, single-point lessons a leader might utilize to start a staff meeting, etc., and can be utilized across a range of delivery modalities. That way, the chief learning officer has access to whatever tools he or she needs in whatever circumstances arise. *"Here's the whole library! How can we help you resolve whatever jobs arise in your life this year?"*

FranklinCovey also sells entire *processes* and experiences geared toward satisfying a particular Job to Be Done. At a high level, the offerings are grouped around various categories of jobs—for example leadership, execution, customer loyalty, sales performance—but underneath each of those categories are offerings aimed at specific Jobs to Be Done. Jobs that are measured in business outcomes.

For example, after being hired by a major information technology equipment company to help improve sales, FranklinCovey created an offering that not only included training, but also included stationing a full-time coach at the client's headquarters to ensure that the process improvements were adhered to for all sales prospects above $500 million. "A company doesn't get a lot of 'at bats' with contracts of that size," Whitman says. "So we own the outcomes with them. Our deliverable is really a process, not a product." One with measurable ROI.

What has innovating around jobs meant for FranklinCovey? Among other critical shifts in perspective, it's changing the competitive landscape. No longer is it simply competing against other companies that provide world-class training content. It's largely competing in its own lane.

"We try to position ourselves around jobs that don't have competitors," Whitman says. If a company is looking to change its strategy, that work usually goes to a conventional consulting firm. But if they want help in implanting that strategy, getting large numbers of people to do something better or more consistently in order to invariably execute on a new strategy or to achieve a very specific business goal like increasing complex, multimillion-dollar sales, FranklinCovey sees few competitors for the gig.

In fact, Whitman says, traditional consulting firms have become a source of work for them—FranklinCovey's been retained to help see a new strategy through. As we'll discuss later in the book, competitive advantage is built not just by understanding customers' jobs, but by creating the experiences that customers seek both in purchasing and using the product or service—and then, crucially, building internal processes to ensure that those experiences are reliably delivered to the customer every time. That is what's hard for competitors to copy.

And that means the potential for growth is far greater than it was when FranklinCovey was only competing with other providers of training products. In 2015 FranklinCovey's revenue reached $220 million, a 9.2 percent compounded annual growth rate in the past six years.

HALF THE FUNCTIONALITY AT TWICE THE PRICE

Intuit cofounder Scott Cook was an early adopter of Jobs Theory—and his work has helped define and shape the theory. Within Intuit he refers to the "improvement in the customer's life that matters most to him in selecting the product." But we agree that we're talking about the same thing: the progress a customer seeks in particular circumstances. He and I eventually went on to coauthor the first article to preview the Theory of Jobs to Be Done in *Harvard Business Review*[2] (along with one of the coauthors of this book, Taddy Hall). This theory helped Intuit launch the wildly successful QuickBooks accounting software for the small business market—and has guided the company's innovation strategy since.

Interestingly, Cook says he nearly missed the insight that led to QuickBooks—a product that has become critical to Intuit's long-term growth beyond its original offering—because he wasn't focused on the right things. For years small business customers were using Intuit's *personal* financial software product, Quicken, to jury-rig a way to keep track of small business accounts—a workaround that made no sense. Quicken didn't allow small business customers to do a whole host of things that other successful business software on the market already did, such as keeping journals, ledgers, postings, closings, debits, and credits, and to do so in the recognized language of accountants. Why were these folks using Quicken when there was far more sophisticated accounting software easily available to them?

It turns out that accounting software was the last thing these people wanted. They just wanted to have the confidence that financial mechanics were operating efficiently—invoices sent, cash collected, and bills paid. The progress they wanted to make was more about what they *didn't* want to do than what they did.

What Cook and his team identified was the difference between a task (enter a debit in the ledger) and a genuine struggle—in *specific circumstances*. These business owners didn't need to understand the complexities of recognized standards of accounting. "'Civilians' don't know that stuff," Cook recalls. They just wanted to get money in and out of their business as efficiently as possible. "We did all the hocus-pocus in the background," he explains. So if a small business owner wanted to pay a bill, she'd see a check on the screen and didn't have to work through confusing and cumbersome accounting language. "And if she wanted to see which customers were late in paying, we made that fast and easy."

It became clear that Intuit's competitors for this Job to Be Done were not the other sophisticated accounting software products already on the market, but rather the decision whether to hire another person just to do the books, spending extra hours at the office just to get the paperwork done, figuring out how to construct and use one of the generic spreadsheet software products available, or even a shoebox where all the receipts went with no hope of ever actually being properly reconciled. Thus, the size of the potential market couldn't even be accurately estimated based on current sales of competing software. Intuit was seizing the opportunity for people who had not found any satisfactory solution at all yet—a much bigger potential market.

To outside eyes, QuickBooks might have seemed an unlikely success. After all, the product offered *half* the functionality of more sophisticated accounting software at *twice* the price. But QuickBooks quickly became—and has remained—the global leader in online accounting software. Competitors were focused on making the best *accounting* software possible. Cook and his team focused on the job customers were trying to do.

A clear view of customers' jobs means an organization should never overshoot what those customers are actually willing to pay for. On the contrary, we believe that when customers find the right product to respond to their Job to Be Done, they're often willing to pay *more*—something we'll demonstrate throughout this book. Intuit's $4 billion in revenue and $25 billion in market cap makes clear that Cook and his team understand that. "All that we do is focus on solving the customers' struggle," Cook says. "That's all we do and the only thing we do."

"WE *GET* YOU"

Intuit may have stumbled into Jobs to Be Done, but the initial discovery of a job doesn't have to be accidental or random. With a deep understanding of this theory, organizations have the ability to fundamentally change the way they innovate and grow. So many innovations that are launched with great hope and fanfare flop because they have focused on improving the product on dimensions that are irrelevant to the consumer's actual Job to Be Done, with enormous resources wasted in the process. This is because improvements on such dimensions do not *cause* a customer to pull that product into his life. A product that has been designed specifically to fulfill a well-understood Job to Be Done allows you to crawl into the skin of your customer and see the world through her eyes. It says to the customer, "We *get* you."

But as we'll discuss throughout this book, uncovering an unsatisfactorily resolved job is only the first step. Your organization has to build the right set of experiences in how customers find, purchase, and use your product or service—and integrate all the corresponding processes to ensure that those experiences are consistently delivered. When you are solving a customer's job, your products essentially become *services*. What matters is not the bundle of product attributes you rope together, but the *experiences* you enable to help your customers make the progress they want to make.

We believe the thinking in this book has the potential to change not just innovation success rates, but to transform companies themselves. But first, executives have to change what they believe is possible. For far too long, companies have accepted that innovation success is just random and we've allowed ourselves failure rates that we wouldn't tolerate in any other aspect of business. Innovation does not have to be the least successful thing that companies do.

- Organizations that lack clarity on what the real jobs their customers hire them to do can fall into the trap of providing one-size-fits-all solutions that ultimately satisfy no one.
- Deeply understanding jobs opens up new avenues for growth and innovation by bringing into focus distinct "jobs-based" segments—including groups of "nonconsumers" for which an acceptable solution does not currently exist. They choose to hire nothing, rather than something that does the job poorly. Nonconsumption has the potential to provide a very, very big opportunity.
- Seeing your customers through a jobs lens highlights the real competition you face, which often extends well beyond your traditional rivals.

- What jobs are *your* customers hiring your products and services to get done?
- Are there segments with distinct jobs that you are inadequately serving with a one-size-fits-none solution?
- Are your products—or competitors'—overshooting what customers are actually willing to pay for?
- What experiences do customers seek in order to make progress—and what obstacles must be removed for them to be successful?
- What does your understanding of your customers' Jobs to Be Done reveal about the *real* competition you are facing?

NOTES

1. I have served on the board of trustees of SNHU in the past and on the FranklinCovey board since 2004.
2. Christensen, Clayton M., Scott Cook, and Taddy Hall. "Marketing Malpractice: The Cause and the Cure." *Harvard Business Review*, December 2005. https://hbr.org/2005/12/marketing-malpractice-the-cause-and-the-cure.

SECTION 2

THE HARD WORK—AND PAYOFF—OF APPLYING JOBS THEORY

I went in thinking we were in the business of new home construction. But I realized we were instead in the business of moving lives.

—BOB MOESTA

CHAPTER 4

Job Hunting

THE BIG IDEA

So where are all these jobs just waiting to be discovered— and how do you find them? The solution lies not in the tools you're using, but what you are looking for and how you piece your observations together. If you can spot barriers to progress or frustrating experiences, you've found the first clues that an innovation opportunity is at hand. We offer here a sampling of ways to uncover jobs: seeing jobs in your own life, finding opportunity in "nonconsumption," identifying workarounds, zoning in on things you don't want to do, and spotting unusual uses of products. Innovation is less about producing something new and more about enabling something new and important for customers. Here's how job hunting works.

A decade ago, Bob Moesta was charged with helping bolster sales of new homes and condominiums for a midsize Detroit-area building company in an increasingly difficult market. The company had targeted downsizers—retirees looking to move out of the family home and divorced single parents. The units they had developed were priced to appeal to that segment—$120,000 to $200,000—with high-end touches to give a sense of luxury. "Squeakless" floors. Triple waterproof basements with Tyvek brand wrapping. Granite counters and stainless steel appliances. Buyers had the ability to customize every detail imaginable—from the knobs on cabinets to the tiles in the bathroom; the company offered a thirty-page checklist of choices to be made. A well-staffed sales team was available six days a week for any prospective buyer who walked in the door. A generous ad campaign was splashed across the relevant Sunday real estate sections.

But in spite of having lots of traffic to their units, few visits ended up converting to a sale. Maybe bay windows would be better? Throw in a few other bells and whistles? Focus group participants thought all those things sounded good. So the architect scrambled to add in bay windows to a few showcase units. But still sales did not improve. The company was stumped as to how to change its trajectory. The Detroit-area real estate market was troubled long before many other areas of the country felt the pinch. With an auto industry that had been hemorrhaging jobs for decades, Detroit's unemployment rate in the mid-2000s was among the worst in the country—nearly three times the national average. And with its investment in building new homes in fourteen different locations in a difficult market, the company needed to close sales quickly.

Although the company had calculated the cost-benefit analysis of all the details in each unit, it actually had very little idea what made the difference between attracting a tire-kicker and a serious buyer. It was easy to speculate about myriad reasons for poor sales: bad weather, underperforming salespeople, the looming recession, holiday slowdowns, competitors' offerings, and the condos' location. The focus had been all about what else they could add to the condos to make them appeal to buyers and that was not working.

But Moesta took a different approach: he set out to learn what job the condominium was hired to do for people who had already bought a unit. "I asked people to draw a timeline of how they got here," he recalls. The first thing he learned, piecing together patterns in scores of interviews, was what could *not* explain who was most likely to buy. There wasn't a clear demographic or even psychographic profile for one of the company's new-home buyers—even though they could be lumped into a segment of downsizers. There wasn't a definitive set of features in the new homes that buyers had valued so much that it tipped their decision making. In fact, these features actually provided an obstacle: it was overwhelming to have to pick every single detail of a new home.

But the conversations revealed an unusual clue: the dining room table. Though prospective customers who came through the units repeatedly told the company they wanted a big living room, a large second bedroom for guests and visitors, and a breakfast bar to make entertaining company easy and casual, they were stressed about what to do with their existing dining room table. "They kept saying, 'As soon as I could figure out what to do with my dining room table, then I was free to move.'" Moesta and his colleagues couldn't quite understand why the dining room table was such a big deal. In most cases people were referring to well-used, out-of-date furniture that might best be given to charity—or relegated to the local dump.

But as Moesta sat at his own dining room table with his family over Christmas, he suddenly understood. Every birthday was spent around that table. Every Christmas. Homework was spread out on the table. The children had made forts under it. Even the dings and scratches all had a story. The table represented family. The life they had built together. "That was a 'wow!' moment for me," he recalls. "I realized that was huge."

What was stopping buyers from making the decision to move was not something that the construction company had failed to offer, but rather the anxiety that came from giving up something that had profound meaning. One interviewee talked about needing days—and multiple boxes of tissues—to clean out just one closet in her house in preparation for the move. Every decision about what she had enough space to keep in the new location was emotional. Old photos. Children's first-grade art projects. Scrapbooks. "She was reflecting on her life," Moesta says. "Every choice felt like she was discarding a memory."

That realization helped Moesta and his team begin to understand the struggle these potential home buyers faced. "I went in thinking we were in the business of new home construction," recalls Moesta. "But I realized we were instead in the business of moving lives."

With this understanding of the Job to Be Done, dozens of small, but important, changes were made to the offering. For example, the architect managed to create space in the units for a classic dining room table by reducing the size of the second bedroom by 20 percent. The company also focused on helping buyers with the anxiety of the move itself, which included providing moving services, two years of storage, and a sorting room space on the premises where new owners could take their time making decisions about what to keep and what to discard without the pressure of a looming move. Instead of thirty pages of customized choices, which actually overwhelmed buyers, the company offered three variations of finished units—a move that quickly reduced the "cold feet" contract cancellations from five or six a month to one. And so on.

Everything was designed to signal to buyers: we get you. We understand the progress you're trying to make and the struggle to get there. Understanding the job enabled the company to get to the *causal mechanism* of why its customers might pull this solution into their lives. It was complex, but not complicated. That, in turn, allowed the housing company to differentiate its offering in ways competitors weren't likely to copy—or even understand. A jobs perspective changed everything. The company actually *raised*

$3,500 (profitably), which included covering the cost of moving and storage.

By 2007, when sales in the industry were off by 49 percent and the market all around them was plummeting, the developers had actually grown the business 25 percent.

Jobs Theory is an integration tool—a way to make sense of the complex amalgam of needs that are driving consumer choices in particular circumstances. It tells you which pieces of information are needed, how they relate to one another, and how they can be used to create solutions that perfectly nail the job. Jobs Theory is effective because it focuses you on the *right* complexity, breaking it down into elements you need to understand for successful innovation. It's the difference between having a full, comprehensive narrative versus a few scattered frames of the movie, randomly selected as highlights. Jobs to Be Done tell the whole story.

WHERE ARE THE JOBS?

So where are all these jobs just waiting to be discovered?

In what follows we provide some guidance to would-be job hunters by sharing some of the insights and approaches we've found to be useful over many years of working with companies on real-world innovation challenges. We are not attempting to be comprehensive or provide a step-by-step manual. Indeed, as we'll stress throughout this book, we don't believe there is any *one* right way to identify Jobs to Be Done. We've chosen to include here some ideas that may provide a different view through a jobs lens. As Amazon founder Jeff Bezos is fond of quoting, "Perspective is worth 80 I.Q. points."

Some of the most significant advances in science come on the heels of bright minds observing all the same things, with all the same tools, for years and years before someone with fresh eyes comes with a breakthrough. Thomas Kuhn, the influential philosopher and scientific historian explores this phenomenon in *The*

Structure of Scientific Revolutions. These breakthrough moments, he concludes, represent a "paradigm shift" where "Scientists see new and different things when looking with familiar instruments in places they have looked before."

The same is true when uncovering jobs: the problem lies not in the tools you're using, but what you are looking for and how you piece your observations together. Jobs analysis doesn't require you to throw out the data and research you have already gathered. Personas, ethnographic research, focus groups, customer panels, competitive analysis, and so on, can all be perfectly valid starting points for uncovering important insights—if you're looking with the right lenses.

Remember the thought-exercise of making a minidocumentary we discussed in chapter 2? You're trying to capture the story of customers in their moments of struggle or desire for progress. A jobs lens changes what you see: the priorities and tradeoffs that customers are willing to make may look completely different, the competitive landscape shifts to a surprising cast of characters, and opportunity for growth appears where none might have seemed possible. Jobs are all around us, but it helps to know where to look and how to interpret what you find. You have to have a job-hunting strategy.

We offer here five ways to uncover jobs that might be right in front of you if you know what you're looking for: seeing jobs in your own life, finding opportunity in nonconsumption, identifying workarounds, zoning in on things we *don't* want to do, and spotting unusual uses of products. Here's how that works:

I. FINDING A JOB CLOSE TO HOME

In the context of a data-obsessed world, it might be a surprise that some of the world's greatest innovators have succeeded with little more than their own intuition about a Job to Be Done to guide their efforts. Sony founder Akio Morita actually advised against market research, urging instead to "carefully watch how people live, get an intuitive sense as to what they might want and then go with it." Sony's breakthrough Walkman cassette player was temporarily put on hold when market research indicated that consumers would never buy a tape player that didn't have the capacity to record and that customers would be irritated by the use of earphones. But Morita ignored his marketing department's warning, trusting his own gut instead. The Walkman went on to sell over 330 million units and created a worldwide culture of personal music devices.

Understanding the unresolved jobs in your own life can provide fertile territory for innovation. Just look in the mirror—your life is very articulate. If it matters to you, it's likely to matter to others. Take the example of Khan Academy founder Sal Khan's initial amateur YouTube videos to help explain math to his young cousin. They weren't even something new—there were hundreds of other online math tutorials on YouTube alone. Most of them looked and sounded better. "They weren't using a USB headset like I was," he recalls. "My version was cheap and dirty." But there was one key difference. The other lessons felt complicated and pedantic. "They weren't focusing on the core conceptual ideas—and they definitely weren't fun," he says. Not that his cousin could have told him that. "She was 12. I don't know how introspective she was about the process," he recalls. Khan's cousin Nadia had found the way math was taught in her classroom at school stressful—as were the options of having her parents try their best to help her understand or asking the teacher for extra help. But with her cousin's online videos, the stakes were low. Khan created his videos not simply to teach his cousin math, but to help him stay connected to his family and share his own love of learning. His cousin, on the other hand, hired his videos to feel successful by being able to learn complex math concepts in a way that was actually fun.[1]

Turns out there were lots of people who felt the same pain as his cousin. Today millions of students all over the world learn at their own pace through Khan Academy online.

Some of the most successful start-ups in recent years have come from the founders' personal Job to Be Done. Sheila Marcelo started Care.com, the online "matchmaking" service for child care, senior care, pet care, and so on, after struggling with her own child-care needs. It now boasts nearly 10 million members across sixteen countries, and revenues approaching $60 million, less than ten years after its founding.

But if you're breaking out in a cold sweat worrying that you haven't had a road-to-Damascus insight like these entrepreneurs, don't worry. The good news is you don't need to rely on personal inspiration to uncover a job that might provide a valuable innovation opportunity for your organization. You can learn a lot just by watching the customers you do—and don't—already have. But you have to know what you're looking for.

2. COMPETING WITH NOTHING

You can learn as much about a Job to Be Done from people who *aren't* hiring any product or service as you can from those who are. We call this "nonconsumption," when consumers can't find any solution that actually satisfies their job and they opt to do nothing instead. Too often, companies consider only how they can grab shares away from competitors, but not where they can find unseen demand. They may not even *see* it at all because existing data isn't going to tell them where to find it. But nonconsumption often represents the most fertile opportunities, as was true for Southern New Hampshire University.

Once a company shakes off the shackles of category-based competition, the market for a breakthrough innovation can be *much* larger than might be assumed from the size of the traditional view of the competitive landscape. You won't see nonconsumption if you're not looking for it.

Chip Conley, Airbnb's head of global hospitality and strategy, says that 40 percent of its "guests" say they would not have made a trip at all—or stayed with family—if Airbnb didn't exist. And virtually all its "hosts" would never have considered renting out a spare room or even their whole home. For these customers, Airbnb is competing with nothing.

Kimberly-Clark already had a huge share of the market for adult incontinence products when it realized there might be opportunity it hadn't seen before. The company's line of Depend products was first introduced in the 1980s, when the company identified the opportunity to solve a painful problem for adults who suffered with incontinence, typically ill or elderly people. It was a very successful product by any measure. But there were still lots of people who would rather make do with nothing than hire Depends.

The company has always been careful to label them "under-garments" on the packaging, but they more or less looked like a bag of adult diapers. They came in bags similar in size and shape to those for children's diapers and were, at least in the beginning, white, bulky, and worst of all, crinkly. (*Saturday Night Live* ran a mocking skit showing adults coaxing their elderly parents into wearing the fictitious "Depend Legends" undergarments, branded with famous faces.)

With the lens of Jobs to Be Done, the company realized there was still an enormous untapped opportunity. Nearly 40 percent of adults over fifty suffer from incontinence, according to Kimberly-Clark's research, a number that is expected to increase with aging populations and longer life expectancies. Research suggests that even though one in three women over the age of eighteen suffers from some sort of incontinence issue, only a small percentage of them use any incontinence product at all. There are many, many consumers who opt for nothing rather than go into a store and purchase an adult diaper. "The stigma and anxiety exact an enormous quality-of-life toll on sufferers," explains Kimberly-Clark's Giuseppina Buonfantino. People typically suffer for as long as two years before giving in and buying an incontinence product at all. In desperation, consumers will turn to any number of workarounds—for example, using feminine hygiene pads as a stop-gap measure. Or most painfully, they simply disengage socially: they don't travel, they stop going to restaurants and shows, stop spending time with their friends and family. There was a very clear Job to Be Done for those people who would rather stay home than risk embarrassment: help them reclaim their lives.

With that insight, Buonfantino says, the company focused its efforts not just on creating a new product—Depend Silhouette Briefs for women and Real Fit Briefs for men—but about breaking the stigma and giving people back some dignity in dealing with the issue. Top of that list was the need to create a product that didn't remotely look or feel like an adult diaper. The new product had to inspire customers to overcome their anxiety about purchasing and wearing an adult undergarment.

This wasn't simply a cosmetic or marketing issue. The company had to create completely new materials and technologies, which would allow it to manufacture a product that looked and felt very similar to normal underwear. The packaging was designed to look like any other underwear purchase—with transparent windows that allowed customers to see that the product itself really looked like underwear.

Having spent the time to understand the required job, including its critical emotional components, the company ultimately delivered a home run. A Nielsen Breakthrough Innovation winner, in its first year, the product generated $60 million in sales, with 30 percent growth in year two—without harming the market share of its existing products. This has led to subsequent international launches—all in a "mature" category.

A jobs perspective can change how you see the world so

significantly that major new growth opportunities arise where none had seemed possible before. In fact, if it feels like there isn't room for growth in a market, it could actually be a signal that you've defined the job poorly. There may be an entirely new growth opportunity right in front of you.

3. WORKAROUNDS AND COMPENSATING BEHAVIORS

As an innovator, spotting consumers who are struggling to resolve a Job to Be Done by cobbling together workarounds or compensating behaviors, as Kimberly-Clark did with Silhouettes, should cause your heart to beat a little faster. You've spotted potential customers—consumers who are so unhappy with the available solutions to a job they very deeply want to solve that they're going to great lengths to create their own solution. Whenever you see a compensating behavior, pay very close attention, because it's likely a clue that there is an innovation opportunity waiting to be seized—one on which customers would place a high value. But you won't even see these anomalies—compensating behavior and cobbled-together workarounds—if you're not *fully immersed in the context of their struggle.*

Frustrated by how ridiculously difficult—and financially punitive—banks had made the experience of opening a savings account for a child, I have a friend who actually went to the extraordinary lengths of setting up a symbolic "Bank of Daddy" to help his children understand the power of compound interest. The children's allowance and pocket money never actually went into a bank—Mom and Dad just kept it for them—but every month the dad would credit their allowance to the account and calculate and add the interest they had accrued, paying a reasonable interest rate, unlike the real bank.

It's no surprise that many people have given up on savings accounts altogether. For decades, traditional banks had made it clear that the segment of "low net worth" individuals who wanted a simple savings account was undesirable. They were unprofitable in banks' existing business models. So the banks did everything in their power to put them off: requiring minimum balances and charging fees and penalties for every conceivable service. My friend's children, with their pocket money and presents from Grammy and Grampy, were not part of a segment banks wanted to attract. But that didn't mean there wasn't a rich opportunity to be mined.

Enter ING Direct, which saw the market through a new lens.

There was a complex Job to Be Done that had little to do with the function of saving money. In my friend's case, he wanted to feel like a good father by helping his children understand the power of saving toward goals. ING Direct took away the obstacles. It's an incredibly simple offering: The bank offers a few savings accounts, a handful of certificates of deposit, and mutual funds. The bank has no deposit minimums—you can open an account with a single dollar, if you want. It's fast, convenient, and more secure than jamming tens and twenties into the back of a drawer, leaving them in birthday cards and forgetting about them—or calculating outsized interest rates at the Bank of Daddy.

ING Direct needed a very different cost structure and business model if it was going to make money—but that was much easier to make work once it understood the job customers were trying to do. Everything about ING Direct corresponded to solving customers' Jobs to Be Done: because it was an online bank, its operating costs were a fraction of those of brick-and-mortar competitors. And it also had none of the overhead costs of specialists for wealth management, loans, international services, and so on. That meant the focus on profitability and efficiency came from a completely different angle—not about the burden of supporting operating costs, but optimizing to solve customers' jobs.

ING Direct swiftly became the fastest-growing bank in the United States. Traditional banks should have had all the tools to capture this market, but they focused instead on segmenting customers instead of understanding their Jobs to Be Done. In 2012 ING Direct was sold to Capital One for $9 billion.

OpenTable, which is an online, real-time restaurant reservation service, was born out of a common workaround. I've always hated having to figure out how to make dinner reservations at a restaurant. When you have two friends in town, you decide you want to go out. You want to show them your favorite restaurant. Everybody checks their schedule and agrees, so you call the restaurant and find out they don't have capacity at the time you agreed with your friends. Can you come at 9:00 instead? So now you have to call your friends back to see if that works. And it turns out, one of them has a babysitting problem. OK, back to the drawing board. What other restaurant should we go to? We've all been doing this workaround to get restaurant reservations for ages, but OpenTable solved this job.

4. LOOK FOR WHAT PEOPLE *DON'T* WANT TO DO

I think I have as many jobs of *not* wanting to do something as ones that I want positively to do. I call them "negative jobs." In my experience, negative jobs are often the best innovation opportunities.

What parent doesn't identify with this struggle: Your child wakes up with a sore throat. Your experience tells you it's probably strep. You want your child to feel better and know that getting medicine in as quickly as possible is key, but gee, it's *really* not a good day for this to happen. It's a busy day at work, the child-care arrangements will be complicated, and the last thing you want to have to do is take time to get to the doctor for what probably will be a quick poke and prod to confirm what you suspect. If you call the pediatrician, he will, in good conscience, say he can't prescribe anything without seeing your child. After finagling your way into an unscheduled appointment, you might sit in that waiting room for a long time until the doctor squeezes you in. Hours after that first call, when you finally get into the exam room, the doctor looks at your child, does a quick culture, and concludes it's strep throat. He'll call something into the pharmacy but you have to wait thirty minutes to pick it up. The whole afternoon is shot. In this case, the Job to Be Done is "I *don't* want to see the doctor."

Harvard Business School alum Rick Krieger and some partners decided to start QuickMedx, the forerunner of CVS Minute-Clinics, after Krieger spent a frustrating few hours waiting in an emergency room for his son to get a strep-throat test. CVS Minute-Clinic can see walk-in patients instantly and nurse practitioners can prescribe medicines for routine ailments, such as conjunctivitis, ear infections, and strep throat. Because most people *don't* want to go to the doctor if they don't have to, there are now more than a thousand MinuteClinic locations inside CVS pharmacy stores in thirty-three states.

5. UNUSUAL USES

You can learn a lot by observing how your customers use your products, especially when they use them in a way that is different from what your company has envisioned. A story I often use to explain to my students how to find jobs that are hidden in plain sight is the case of Church & Dwight's baking soda "category." For nearly a century, the company's iconic orange box of Arm & Hammer baking soda had been a staple in every American kitchen, an essential ingredient for baking. But in the late 1960s, management observed the diverse circumstances for which consumers grabbed that orange box off the shelf. They added it to laundry detergent, mixed it into toothpaste, sprinkled it on the carpet, or left an open box in the refrigerator, as well as other unusual uses. Until then, it hadn't occurred to management that their staple product could possibly be hired for any job other than classic baking. But those observations led to a jobs-based strategy with the introduction of the first phosphate-free laundry detergent and a series of other highly successful new products, such as cat litter, carpet cleaner, air fresheners, deodorant, and so on.

Today, we see the Arm & Hammer brand on a wide range of products—but each responding to a specific Job to Be Done:

> Help my mouth feel fresh and clean
> Deodorize my refrigerator
> Keep my swimming pool clean and fresh for me and my environment
> Help my underarms stay clean and fresh
> Clean and freshen my carpets
> Deodorize that stinky cat litter!
> Freshen the air in this room
> Remove shower stain and mildew

It's not that these jobs were new—they've long existed. Church & Dwight just had to discover them. The orange-box baking-soda business is now less than 7 percent of Arm & Hammer's consumer revenue; observing unusual uses has spawned millions of dollars in new product creations.

Some of the biggest successes in consumer packaged goods in recent years have come not from jazzy new products, but from a job identified through unusual uses of long-established products. For example, NyQuil had been on the market for decades as a cold remedy, but it turned out that some consumers were knocking back a couple of spoonfuls to help them sleep, even when they weren't sick. Hence, ZzzQuil was born, offering consumers the good night's rest they wanted without the other active ingredients they didn't need.

When marketers understand the structure of the market from the customer's Job to Be Done perspective, instead of through product or customer categories, the potential size of the markets they serve suddenly becomes *very* different. Growth can be found where none seemed possible before.

THE "EMOTIONAL SCORE"

We've identified above five different fertile areas to mine for jobs.[2] But to do it properly, once you've found a promising vein, you have to look all around it to understand the *context* of a job before you can innovate to solve it. If you are to create products and services that customers want to pull into their lives, you have to drill deep and look wide, identifying not only the functional, but also the social and emotional dimensions of the progress your customers are trying to make. Even the most experienced innovators can miss rich opportunities that are buried in the context of understanding a job well if their focus is too narrow.

Take, for example, Todd Dunn, who spends a lot of time thinking about what tools doctors need to do their job well. As director of innovation at Intermountain Healthcare Transformation Lab,[3] Dunn is charged with helping drive innovation into all corners of the organization, including rethinking approaches to common practices for caring for patients. But one fall day a few years ago, he found himself in unfamiliar territory: as a patient, being cared for by his employer. Dunn had been nursing a bad knee for far too long and finally decided to have one of Intermountain's top orthopedic surgeons check it out. He'd been in Intermountain's exam rooms many times in the course of his job, but everything about being a patient in that little examination room registered differently on him that day. "I sat in that room, on that crinkly paper, waiting for the doctor—and I thought to myself, who designed this? That crinkly paper is uncomfortable. You don't know if you're going to slide off the table. It makes a noise every time you move. Even though it seems like a small detail, it prevents you from being relaxed. It creates anxiety," Dunn recalls.

As director of hundreds of innovation efforts over his career, he recognized immediately that the paper was designed for function—its purpose was to keep the examining table clean. But from the perspective of being a patient, it actually heightened his sense of being vulnerable. Combined with the sterile lighting in the room, his X-rays already ominously lined up on a light board, and the hushed sounds of people rushing by his door, by the time Dr. Holmstrom came in, Dunn was on edge.

But just minutes into the appointment, Holmstrom eased Dunn's anxiety. As he began to discuss Dunn's prognosis, he grabbed a piece of paper to sketch out, crudely, what was wrong with Dunn's knee and what they could do to fix it. This was comforting, but puzzling. Dunn knew there was state-of-the-art software in that computer just over Holmstrom's shoulder to help him record and communicate his diagnosis during an examination. But the doctor didn't choose to use it. "Why aren't you typing this into the computer?" Dunn asked.

In response, Holmstrom rolled his chair over to the computer to demonstrate. The doctor then explained that not only would typing the information into the computer take him too much time, but it would also cause him to have to turn away from his patient, even just for a few moments, when he was delivering a diagnosis. He didn't want his patients to have that experience. The doctor wanted to maintain eye contact, to keep the patient at ease, to assure him that he was in good hands. In that moment, it wasn't most important to call up a state-of-the-art computer image, but to connect and reassure an anxious patient. "We'd designed a terrific software system that we thought would help this doctor get his job done, but he was choosing to 'hire' a piece of paper and pen instead," Dunn recalls. "It really hit home for me—we'd designed everything in that room from a functional perspective, but we had completely overlooked the emotional score."

Dunn and his team had already been exploring Jobs Theory to goose their innovation, but that visit, as a patient, really brought home the importance of understanding the full complexity of a job with all its social, emotional, and functional dimensions. However state-of-the-art the software tools were, they were missing the complete picture.

Dunn's epiphany as an actual patient helped him understand shortcomings in Intermountain's broader innovation process. Intermountain had historically been heavily reliant on proprietary software for virtually every function in the hospital, from allowing the doctors to order tests and follow-up services for patients to actually scheduling who is in what room at what time. Software development, Dunn says, would often come after, say, bringing clinicians into a conference room and asking them what they need. Analysts would write up what they heard and pass it off to an engineer, who would, in turn, develop a solution that met the clinicians' description. The fundamental assumption, Dunn says, was "the clinician is always right or that the clinician can explain what they do in enough detail to satisfy a 'job' that they need help getting done." So whatever he or she told them needed software to do, that's what the engineers designed it to do.

But somehow, what the clinicians said didn't always match what they actually wanted to do in reality. And they missed a target customer, the patient. Too often, projects required extensive updates or fixes, were delayed, or were canceled altogether. "We had been doing design thinking for a long time," Dunn says. "But things still didn't work. I realized we were observing the people—we could tell you a lot about their behavior and what happened first, what happened second, and so on. But we weren't observing the *job*."

Since then, Intermountain's team has instituted a jobs-based framework (internally known as Design for People) that requires observation and unpacking of not only functional, but also emotional and social components of a job before designing the innovation brief. "We realized people have to have a broader view. It's assumed that 'user experience' is all about a beautiful screen and making sure the buttons are in all the right places. But that has almost nothing to do with getting the experience of using the software right—in the real world where clinicians use it. You can't do design requirements in a conference room. You have to get out in the wild and live it."

Many companies fall into the trap of asking consumers what about their current offering they could tweak to make it more appealing. Faster? More colors? Cheaper? When you start with the assumption that you're just altering what you already have created, or relying on broader industry-accepted category definitions, you may have already missed the opportunity to uncover the real job for consumers.

Procter & Gamble (P&G) learned this the hard way with its initial introduction of disposable diapers into China, which should have been a slam dunk. P&G knew how to make and sell diapers to Western consumers and there were millions of babies in China who, according to local practices, didn't use diapers at all. Wasn't that a market full of potential customers?

"The concept was that if we could produce a diaper inexpensively enough in developing markets, we could grow the market substantially," recalls David Goulait, who spent decades within P&G's world-renowned R&D group. Most of the effort, Goulait recalls, was on how to make "a functional containment device" for a child that would cost only ten cents—dubbed "the ten-cent diaper." The assumption was that parents in China would buy lower-quality versions of US and European diapers if they were affordable enough.

But to P&G's surprise, the cut-price diapers were not flying off the shelves. Realizing he was trying to create a product for a market that did not automatically see the value of traditional diapers—at all—Goulait was eager to find clues as to what was going wrong. He started by researching how developing-market consumers felt about the functional features of the diapers that had always been a source of pride and excellence at P&G. Were the diapers too rough? Too flimsy? Too expensive? It was hard to find an answer. Not speaking the language in the developing countries in which P&G was doing research, Goulait hovered in a back room of a focus group listening in, reliant on his translator. As the moderator worked through the standard protocol of questions—how did the experience go, what was the high point of the week, and so on— one woman's answers caused hearty laughter from the group. What had she said to trigger that response? The translator giggled, too. The highlight of this woman's week, she reported happily, was renewed intimacy with her husband—three times in that one week.

How did that relate to the diaper? Because the baby had slept through the night, she, too, could sleep through the night. In turn, she found herself more rested. The rest of the story then made sense. The moderator then asked her what her husband thought about the diaper. "That was the best ten cents he ever spent. . . ." More laughter.

In that moment, Goulait realized that his approach had been too narrow, as it had been constrained primarily to the functional characteristics of the diaper. But the Job to Be Done solved by the diaper was more complex and interesting than that; it included social dimensions related to its impact on a couple's home life and relationship and various emotional dimensions as well. For Goulait the lens of Jobs to Be Done provided a kind of missing link. "Prior to that," Goulait recalls of his conversion to the power of Jobs Theory, "we had a very strong consumer insights-construct framed around the idea of 'consumer need.' Our approach was very much about defining those needs through typical market research and then delivering against them."

But in Goulait's view, the "needs" being identified were too often limited exclusively to "functional" needs without taking into account the broader social and emotional dimensions of a customer's struggle. "And the idea that in many cases emotional and social could be on the same plane as functional needs—and maybe even be a driver . . . ," Goulait says. "For me that was the 'aha!' Let's not separate those three things. They're integrated. They are, in fact, the key to making a really successful product introduction." Jobs to Be Done provided not just the language, but the *construct*—the idea that you have to understand and innovate around all three dimensions of a customer's job. "We *kind of* knew that, but we didn't have the construct and language to address it specifically and to really make it actionable."

So P&G worked to make sure that potential customers would recognize how its diapers truly solved the full Job to Be Done in their lives. With the help of a two-year research project with the Beijing Children's Hospital's Sleep Research Center, P&G reported that the babies who wore Pampers disposable diapers fell asleep 30 percent faster and slept an extra thirty minutes every night. The study even made a connection between extra sleep and improved cognitive development, a significant benefit in a culture that places a high premium on academic achievement. When P&G eventually relaunched the diapers in China, the ads featured the explicit emotional and social benefit—research that suggested babies who get a good night's sleep develop better.

By 2013 Pampers was a top-selling diaper brand in China,[4] racking up an estimated $1.6 billion in diaper sales and roughly 30 percent of the market in a country that hadn't used disposable diapers just a decade before.

If a consumer doesn't see his job in your product, it's already game over. Even worse—if a consumer hires your product for reasons other than its intended Job to Be Done, you risk alienating that consumer forever. As we'll discuss more later, it's actually important to signal "this product is not for you" or they'll come back and say it's a crummy product.

METHOD TO THE MADNESS

Where was the stroke of genius in all these success stories? It's in knowing what to look for. There is a method to the madness. What they have in common is the search for *cause*. With a theory to predict what will cause what to happen, breakthrough innovations do not require getting lucky. They don't rely on someone fiddling with a microwave-emitting magnetron and accidentally discovering the chocolate bar in his pocket has suddenly melted or any of the other magical alchemy of brilliance and accidents that have become innovator lore. The magic of the Jobs to Be Done lens is that there isn't any magic required at all. The lens allows you to look at the same things everyone else is looking at—but enables you to *see* differently.

CHAPTER TAKEAWAYS

- Jobs Theory provides a clear guide for successful innovation because it enables a full, comprehensive insight into all the information you need to create solutions that perfectly nail the job.
- There are many ways to develop a deep understanding of the job, including traditional market research techniques. While it's helpful to develop a "job hunting" strategy, what matters most is not the specific techniques you use, but the questions you ask in applying them and how you piece the resulting information together.
- A valuable source of jobs insights is your own life. Our lives are very articulate and our own experiences offer fertile ground for uncovering Jobs to Be Done. Some of the most successful innovations in history have derived from the experiences and introspection of individuals.
- While most companies spend the bulk of their market research efforts trying to better understand their current customers, im-

portant insights about jobs can often be gathered by studying people who are *not* buying your products—or anyone else's—a group we call nonconsumers.

- If you observe people employing a workaround or "compensating behavior" to get a job done, pay close attention. It's usually a clue that you have stumbled on to a high-potential innovation opportunity, because the job is so important and they are so frustrated that they are literally inventing their own solution.
- Closely studying *how* customers use your products often yields important insights into the jobs, especially if they are using them in unusual and unexpected ways.
- Most companies focus disproportionately on the functional dimensions of their customers' jobs; but you should pay equally close attention to uncovering the emotional and social dimensions, as addressing all three dimensions is critical to your solution nailing the job.

QUESTIONS FOR LEADERS

- What are the important, unsatisfied jobs in your own life, and in the lives of those closest to you? Flesh out the circumstances of these jobs, and the functional, emotional, and social dimensions of the progress you are trying to make—what innovation opportunities do these suggest?
- If you are a consumer of your own company's products, what jobs do you use them to get done? Where do you see them falling short of perfectly nailing your jobs, and why?
- Who is ***not*** consuming your products today? How do their jobs differ from those of your current customers? What's getting in the way of these nonconsumers using your products to solve their jobs?

- Go into the field and observe customers using your products. In what circumstances do they use them? What are the functional, emotional, and social dimensions of the progress they are trying to make? Are they using them in unexpected ways? If so, what does this reveal about the nature of their jobs?

NOTES

1. In *Disrupting Class,* which I wrote with my colleagues Michael Horn
    and Curtis Johnson, we assert that going to school isn't a job. The
    job in every student's life is "I want to feel successful every day."
    And, frankly, most schools are not designed to do that job well. In
    fact, kids often come home at the end of a school day feeling intellec-
    tually beat up—that they have failed. Students can hire school to get
    the job done, but there are lots of competitors they could hire. If a
    student isn't feeling successful, for example, he could fire school and
    hire a gang instead. She could get some kind of unskilled job to earn
    money and buy a car to feel successful. These are the "Snickers" and
    "doughnuts" that compete against school and they are very tempt-
    ing to students for whom school is not doing the job. Christensen,
    Clayton M., Michael B. Horn, and Curtis W. Johnson. *Disrupting
    Class: How Disruptive Innovation Will Change the Way the World
    Learns.* New York: McGraw-Hill, 2008.

    By contrast, I'm fascinated by the approach that Khan Academy
    is designing into its offerings. Much of the Khan Academy's mate-
    rial is organized so you *cannot* fail. When a student gets stuck on a
    problem, there are resources easily available to help her understand
    the concept better. If the student gets frustrated and wants to skip to
    the next problem, she can't. She can't advance to the next challenge
    until she understands the current problem. Further resources and
    hints are available with a click of the mouse, enabling the student to
    overcome the challenge and feel like a success.

2. I like to think of this as a kind of "fracking" for jobs. In oil drilling,
    fracking allows companies to become far more productive in their
    attempts to find oil. Before fracking technology was available, com-
    panies had to pick and choose where to drill. If a vein did not yield
    oil, they simply moved on. They could have been very close to oil,
    but if their particular vein did not directly reach into a source, the
    vein was unsuccessful. With fracking, companies are able to drill

very, very deep, but then are able to expand their search horizontally once they're down there when fracturing fluid is pumped at high pressures into the hole to find and widen cracks. This enables far more productive oil drilling. "Fracking" for jobs will do the same.

3. Intermountain Healthcare is a not-for-profit on whose board of trustees I voluntarily serve.

4. The ripple effect of Kimberly-Clark's incontinence products and P&G's diapers in China is enormous. Think of how the lives of family, friends, and colleagues around those who actually use the products are improved, too.

CHAPTER 5

How to Hear What Your Customers Don't Say

THE BIG IDEA

Most companies want to stay closely connected to their customers to make sure they're creating the products and services those customers want. Rarely, though, can customers articulate their requirements accurately or completely—their motivations are more complex and their pathways to purchase more elaborate than they can describe. But you can get to the bottom of it. What they **hire**—and equally important, what they **fire**—tells a story. That story is about the functional, emotional, and social dimensions of their desire for progress—and what prevents them from getting there. The challenge is in becoming part sleuth and part documentary filmmaker—piecing together clues and observations—to reveal the jobs customers are trying to get done.

Pleasant Rowland did absolutely no research when she was considering founding what would become the American Girl doll company back in 1985. She endured one—and only one—focus group in the process of starting the company after her first director of marketing insisted that she had to see one. Sitting behind the two-way glass mirror, she watched as a roundtable of mothers of preteens curled up their lips when the interviewer explained the concept—dolls based in historical periods with books and accessories to support their "stories." "To the person, they said, 'My daughter would never like anything like that, based in history. And all those accessories would just get caught in the vacuum cleaner,'" Rowland recalls. Luckily, Rowland was more confident in her own sense of the Job to Be Done. The company was so successful that she sold it to Mattel thirteen years later for a staggering $700 million.

Consumers can't always articulate what they want. And even when they do, their actions may tell a different story. If I asked you if you care about being environmentally friendly, most of us would say yes. We'd talk about how we recycle or walk instead of driving whenever possible. But if I opened your cupboards, would they tell the same story? How many new parents do you know who say they care about climate change, but gratefully stock disposable diapers instead of cloth? Do you happily pop a plastic K-cup into your coffee machine? On the other hand, research has consistently shown that a significant portion of customers are willing to pay more for foods that are labeled "organic," a word that is so generically used that it's almost meaningless. What explains the disparity? No one aspires to be environmentally unfriendly, but when the actual decision to pull a product into your life has to be made, you pick the solution that best represents the values and tradeoffs you care about *in those particular circumstances.*

OK, so if what consumers say is unreliable, can't you just look at the data instead? Isn't that objective? Well, data is prone to misinterpretation. Sales and marketing data in the toy industry told Pleasant Rowland that girls between the ages of seven and twelve would never play with dolls. And most data only tracks one of the two important moments in a customer's decision to hire a product or service. The most commonly tracked is what we call the "Big Hire"—the moment you buy the product. But there's an equally important moment that doesn't show up in most sales data: when you actually "consume" it.

The moment a consumer brings a purchase into his or her home or business, that product is still waiting to be hired again—we call this the "Little Hire." If a product really solves the job, there will be many moments of consumption. It will be hired again and again. But too often the data companies gather reflects only the Big Hire, not whether it meets customers' Jobs to Be Done in reality. My wife may buy a new dress, but she doesn't really consume it until she's actually cut the tag off and worn it. It's less important to know that she chose blue over green than it is to understand why she made the decision to finally wear it over all other options. How many apps do you have on your phone that seemed like a good idea to download, but you've more or less never used them again? If the app vendor simply tracks downloads, it'll have no idea whether its app is doing a good job solving your desire for progress or not.

Jobs to Be Done have always existed. Innovations have just gotten better and better in the way we can respond to them. So no matter how new or revolutionary your product idea may be, the circumstances of struggle already exist. Consequently, in order to hire your new solution, by definition customers must fire some current compensating behavior or suboptimal solution—including firing the solution of doing nothing at all. Wristwatches were fired in droves as soon as people began carrying mobile phones that not only told them the time, but could sync with calendars and provide alarms and reminders. I fired my weekly *Sports Illustrated* when I could suddenly flip on ESPN. The people who hired Depend Silhouette incontinence products fired staying at home instead of risking going out. Companies don't think about this enough. *What has to get fired for my product to get hired?* They think about making their product more and more appealing, but not what it will be replacing.

A customer's decision-making process about what to fire and

hire has begun long before she enters a store—and it's complicated. There are always two opposing forces battling for dominance in that moment of choice and they both play a significant role.

- **The forces compelling change to a new solution:** First of all, the push of the situation—the frustration or problem that a customer is trying to solve—has to be substantial enough to cause her to want to take action. A problem that is simply nagging or annoying might not be enough to trigger someone to do something differently. Secondly, the pull of an enticing new product or service to solve that problem has to be pretty strong, too. The new solution to her Job to Be Done has to help customers make progress that will make their lives better. This is where companies tend to focus their efforts, asking about features and benefits, and they think, reasonably, that this is the roadmap for innovation. How do we make our product incredibly attractive to hire?
- **The forces opposing change:** There are two unseen, yet incredibly powerful, forces at play at the same time that many companies ignore completely: the forces holding a customer back. First, "habits of the present" weigh heavily on consumers. *"I'm used to doing it this way."* Or living with the problem. *"I don't love it, but I'm at least comfortable with how I deal with it now."* And potentially even more powerful than the habits of the present is, second, the "anxiety of choosing something new." *"What if it's not better?"*

Consumers are often stuck in the habits of the present—the thought of switching to a new solution is almost too overwhelming. Sticking with the devil they know, even if imperfect, is bearable. I refused to upgrade my mobile phone for years, in spite of all the whiz-bang things my assistant assured me the new phone could do, because I was *comfortable* with the one I had. This is largely because—as Nobel Prize winner Daniel Kahneman has shown—the principal pull of the old is that it requires no deliberation and has some intuitive plausibility as a solution already. Loss aversion—people's tendency to want to avoid loss—is twice as powerful psychologically as the allure of gains, as demonstrated by Kahneman and Amos Tversky.[1]

The anxieties that come into play are powerful: anxiety about the cost, anxiety of learning something new, and anxiety of the unknown can be overwhelming. Why do many consumers hang on to their old mobile phones, even when they might get some trade-in value toward a new one? *"What if the new one fails at some point?" "What if I find myself in some kind of unanticipated situation where I need a backup phone?" "What if . . . ?"* Health clubs have only recently come around to the idea that locking customers into annual contracts creates so much anxiety that it prevents them from joining in the first place. Innovators all too often focus exclusively on the forces pushing for change—making sure that the new solution for resolving a customer's struggle is sufficiently alluring to cause them to switch. But they completely ignore the powerful forces blocking that change.

ING Direct went to the extraordinary lengths of opening "cafés" in locations across the United States and Canada to relieve customers' anxiety about a virtual bank. You can drop into one of the cafés, but you can't actually perform any traditional teller-based cash transactions. You can talk to a staff member or use the ATM, but the café's primary purpose is to reassure consumers that it's a "real" bank—and build the brand with its presence. The fact that SNHU is a not-for-profit—with a genuine campus—reduces online students' anxiety that it's some kind of fly-by-night focused on fleecing every possible dollar from unwitting students. Overcoming customer anxieties is a very big deal.

Think of it this way: the job has to have sufficient magnitude to cause people to change their behavior—*"I'm struggling and I want a better solution than I can currently find"*—but the pull of the new has to be much greater than the sum of the inertia of the old and the anxieties about the new. There's almost always some friction associated with switching from one product to another, but it's also almost always discounted by innovators who are sure that their product is so fabulous it will erase any such concerns. It's easy to fire things that simply offer functional solutions to a job. But when the decision involves firing something that has emotional and social dimensions to solving the job, that something is far harder to let go. No matter how frustrated we are with our current situation or how enticing a new product is, if the forces that pull us to hiring something don't outweigh the hindering forces, *we won't even consider hiring something new.*

The progress customers are trying to make has to be understood *in context.* I can't think of a clearly defined job in which the emotional and social forces—and the forces compelling and opposing change—are not critically important. Customers are always reluctant to fire something until they are sure they have something better, even if they're firing simply living with an imperfect solution. This is true even in the B2B arena, where you might think the constraints of a procurement process would leave little room for emotional and social factors—and anxieties and habits of the present. But think about the plant manager making a decision to purchase parts or supplies. It's critically important to her that she can count on having the supplies she needs, when she needs them. Worrying about that will cause sleepless nights, and possibly even career anxiety. Or think about the first-time project manager charged with managing an outside consulting firm. He's going to want to look good to his peers and managers. He wants to be seen to manage the project on budget, on time, and to have developed a strong problem-solving relationship with the consulting firm.

One company that has taken this to heart is Mercer, which my coauthor David Duncan worked with as it sought to create new businesses to drive growth. When Jacques Goulet became global president of the retirement business for Mercer in 2013, the future looked challenging. For decades, Mercer, a global human-resources and financial-services consulting firm, has helped its client companies design retirement plans for their employees and it had grown into a significant portion of their business. But with companies increasingly shifting from defined-benefit plans (in which the company guarantees a company-funded pension for eligible employees) to plans in which the employee makes the majority of investment in his or her own retirement plan (such as a 401(k)), Mercer's primary source of profit in that division looked to be fading away. The company had to start innovating—fast—or face an uncertain future.

For Mercer, simply asking new questions about client jobs triggered a series of important and fresh perspectives on innovation opportunities with its clients. One insight was that Mercer had traditionally thought narrowly about what it was providing for its corporate customers in the past: good advice to its thirty thousand corporate customers that offer retirement plans to their employees. This framing, while narrow, had enabled Mercer to build a large business in the retirement space. But that wasn't going to help Mercer grow now.

What job were clients *really* hiring Mercer to do? Did those pension plans actually solve the full set of customer jobs? On the surface, the heads of corporate finance or human resources were focused on finding a plan to offer employees retirement benefits. But there was more to their job than that. What obstacles were getting in their way?

Goulet's team identified an opportunity for innovation in many organizations' desire to shift from the traditional defined-benefits pension plan to an employee-contribution plan—or get rid of the pension plan altogether by selling it to an insurance company that would take over running it. Leading such an enormous shift, efficiently and with an array of appealing new investment opportunities and benefits for employees, could be overwhelming for human resources or finance professionals. These professionals wanted to be seen to be careful, thoughtful, and navigating an appropriate amount of risk—but also competent enough to make recommendations. And whatever they eventually picked, they didn't want to end up fielding an endless stream of complaints and maintenance for their company.

Historically, the process of identifying new opportunities for what could be hundreds of millions of dollars' worth of pension liabilities had traditionally been time consuming and labor intensive for the HR team or CFO, and not terribly transparent—it was a process that would have increased anxiety for the professionals trying to lead the decision making for their companies. Mercer might approach a handful of insurers on behalf of those clients, provide them some specifics of the client's situation, and then wait for a quote on how much they would charge to take over responsibility for the pension plan. After some back-and-forth, Mercer would present the company with a shortlist of choices and expect it to pick one and carry out the changeover. The process of deciding who to go with and then executing the pension fund buyout could take up to six months, during which time the market, and value of the existing pension fund, might have fluctuated enormously. It was a high-stress process for the HR or finance professional to work through—and their personal reputation could hang on the path they'd recommend.

"That individual has to answer to his boss, who has to answer to the board of directors, who will ask very specific questions about the direction of the pension plan and options," explains Goulet. "The CFO wants to be seen to be very prepared—to have left no stone unturned. If he gets a call from the CEO or the board, he wants to be ready. The emotions very much play into that."

So Mercer's solution reflected that.

With a jobs lens, Mercer's Pension Risk Exchange was born, something akin to a stock exchange where buyers and sellers come to meet and execute and trade in real time. No more long lag times. No more lack of transparency with Mercer in the middle. The process was designed not only to be more productive for clients, but also to include critical elements to help overcome some of the forces that would naturally impede change given the magnitude of the decision involved.

Among the other solutions Mercer baked into its offering: a module that allowed clients to track and model what various buyout options would mean for the company long before they formally engaged in the buyout process. A monitoring function allowed them to model various options and see how they would play out in reality before making a final commitment—a kind of anxiety-reducing practice run.

That has paid off for Mercer. The Pension Risk Exchange has to date launched successfully in the United States, the United Kingdom, and Canada—a tremendous accomplishment for both Mercer and Goulet—and it's a key part of Mercer's ongoing growth strategy. As Goulet puts it: "When we focused on Jobs to Be Done, we realized there was a better mousetrap to be invented."

Jobs Theory helps innovators identify the full picture of the progress a customer is trying to make in particular circumstances, including the complex set of competing needs and relative priorities. You have to understand not only what customers want to hire, but what they'll need to fire to make room for the new solution. All that context matters profoundly. "When we try to answer: *'Is it good enough?'* we're left with opinions and never-ending arguments," explains Chris Spiek, Bob Moesta's partner in the Re-Wired Group. "It's nearly impossible to distinguish between bad, good, good-enough, excellent without the Job to Be Done. When we try to answer: *'Is it good enough to help a consumer make this kind of progress in this kind of situation?'* the answers come easily. The circumstance of the progress they are trying to make is critical to understanding causality."

BUILDING CUSTOMER STORIES

So how can you begin to map out these competing forces to get to the crux of your customers' jobs? Your customers may not be able to tell you what they want, but they can tell you about their struggles.

What are they really trying to accomplish and why isn't what they're doing now working? What is causing their desire for something new? One simple way to think about these questions is through storyboarding. Talk to consumers as if you're capturing their struggle in order to storyboard it later. Pixar has this down to a science: as you piece together your customers' struggle, you can literally sketch out their story:

> *Once upon a time . . .*
> *Every day . . .*
> *One day . . .*
> *Because of that, we did this . . .*
> *Because of this, we did that . . .*
> *Finally I did . . .*

You're building their story, because through that you can begin to understand how the competing forces and context of the job play out for them.

Airbnb's founders clearly understood this. Before launching, the company meticulously identified and then storyboarded forty-five different emotional moments for Airbnb hosts (people willing to rent out their spare room or entire home) and guests. Together, those storyboards almost make up a minidocumentary of the jobs people are hiring Airbnb to do. "When you storyboard something, the more realistic it is, the more decisions you have to make," CEO Brian Chesky told *Fast Company.* "Are these hosts men or women? Are they young, are they old? Where do they live? The city or the countryside? Why are they hosting? Are they nervous? It's not that they [the guests] show up to the house. They show up to the house, how many bags do they have? How are they feeling? Are they tired? At that point you start designing for stuff for a very particular use case."

One of the critical storyboard moments, for example, is the first Little Hire moment for guests—when they first turn up at the home in which they'll stay. How are they greeted? If they're expecting a place that has been described as relaxing, is that evident? Maybe there should be soft music playing or a scented candle, says Airbnb's Chip Conley. Has the host made them feel at ease with their decision? Has the host made clear how they will solve any issues or problems that arise during the stay? And so on. The experience must match the customers' vision of what they hired Airbnb to do. The Airbnb storyboards—which have been constantly tweaked and improved since its founding—reflect the importance of the combination of pushes and pulls that drive their customers' Big Hires and Little Hires.

The moments of struggle, nagging tradeoffs, imperfect experiences, and frustrations in peoples' lives—those are the *what* you're looking for. You're looking for recurring episodes in which consumers seek progress but are thwarted by the limitations of available solutions. You're looking for surprises, unexpected behaviors, compensating habits, and unusual product uses. The *how*—and this is a place where many marketers trip up—are ground-level, granular, extended narratives with a *sample size of one.* Remember, the insights that lead to successful new products look more like a story than a statistic. They're rich and complex. Ultimately, you want to cluster together stories to see if there are similar patterns, rather than break down individual interviews into categories.

THE MATTRESS AGENDA

We'd like to share here a real example of how successful practitioners explore for insights and piece together useful narratives that uncover consumers' jobs. So we asked my colleague Bob Moesta to pick a product everyone would be familiar with. We didn't want to focus on hot new technology or a flashy, hip brand. We wanted vanilla—and he gave us the mattress. Perfect. How could the decision to purchase a mattress be complicated?

The transcript below captures a Jobs to Be Done interview,[2] by Moesta and his colleagues at the Re-Wired Group, of Chicago-based entrepreneur Brian Walker who had just purchased a new mattress. The transcript has been edited for length and clarity, but otherwise unfolds just as the conversation happened live. Its ambling and painstaking deficit-gathering is intentional but it's not a prototype for all customer-research interviews. Our intention in showing it here is to make clear that uncovering the circumstances of a struggle and identifying a Job to Be Done does not require a magical algorithm. There is no one special method of uncovering Jobs to Be Done and that is precisely the point: there is no black box. You just have to have a "beginner's mind" as you walk through a consumer's decision-making process, looking for clues as to the full picture of the struggle.[3]

You might expect a typical interview by a mattress retailer to focus on figuring out which details about the mattress itself led to the decision to buy. *"Was it soft enough? Hard enough? Did it provide the right support? Do you care about the number of coils? Was the color or the pattern on the mattress appealing? What else did you consider buying? How important was price in your decision to buy?"*

But this interview focuses on none of that. Moesta, instead, tries to build a robust picture of the circumstances of the customer's struggle—how he came to think about buying a new mattress. The original goal involves establishing a timeline of all the triggers that actually led to the eventual decision. Walker might appear to be an impulse purchaser. But the backstory that is established, through what might seem to be irrelevant questions, reveals something far more complex. And it is precisely the complexity and the surprising twists and turns that we are seeking.

What is the role that the mattress plays in his life? Why is it important or is it? When is the mattress important and why? Who else is involved in purchase and use of a mattress? What are the barriers and points of friction in buying a new mattress? Depending on the individual's present struggles and desired progress, what alternatives exist to buying a new mattress? Are there occasions in which the individual does not use the mattress when we might expect him to? Conversely, are there moments in life when he uses the mattress in unusual ways? These are just some of the questions we might have as we seek to piece together the richest possible narrative of the mattress-buying process, beginning well before the moment of purchase, ideally when the very first thought of mattress shopping occurred.

THE IMPULSE PURCHASE—THAT WASN'T

INTERVIEWER: The best way to think about this is we're literally filming a documentary. We want all the details around when you first started thinking about buying the mattress, when you made the decision, and then using it and experiencing it for the first time. This is almost investigative: we're building a timeline. Let's just start with when did you buy the mattress?

WALKER: About forty-five days ago. Mid-September.

INTERVIEWER: OK, did you order online, or did you order it . . .

WALKER: I bought it at Costco.

INTERVIEWER: You bought it at Costco, was it weekend, weekday?

WALKER: It was a weekend.

INTERVIEWER: Weekend. Saturday or Sunday?

WALKER: I believe it was a Saturday.

INTERVIEWER: Did you buy anything else with it, or was it just . . .

WALKER: You can never go in Costco and buy just one thing, so yes, I did buy other things.

INTERVIEWER: Did you go with "OK, I'm going to buy this thing today, and oh, I need this and this and this"?

WALKER: No.

INTERVIEWER: You didn't go with the intent to buy it?

WALKER: I did not.

INTERVIEWER: Wow, OK.

INTERVIEWER: What else did you leave with? Do you remember what else you bought in that trip?

WALKER: Well, I have kids, so baby wipes. A lot of milk.

INTERVIEWER: How much milk?

WALKER: You get the thing with the three almond milk thing, and then a couple gallons of something else.

INTERVIEWER: What was the something else?

WALKER: Just the organic, my son has the 2% and my daughter has the non-fat.

INTERVIEWER: Got it, OK.

INTERVIEWER: Did you have a push cart that you started with?

WALKER: Yeah, started with a push cart to get the weekly, the monthly supplies. Paper towels, the milk. The baby wipes.

INTERVIEWER: Anybody with you, or by yourself?

WALKER: We had the whole crew there. My wife and two kids. Family man. This is like "Family Man" inside Costco.

INTERVIEWER: How old are your kids?

WALKER: Four and a half and two.

INTERVIEWER: This is a family experience. Where did you come across the mattress? Early on or later?

WALKER: Towards the end of the forty-five minutes we were in Costco.

INTERVIEWER: Forty-five minutes in Costco.

INTERVIEWER: Was your cart full at that point?

WALKER: Pretty full.

INTERVIEWER: With what else?

WALKER: The milk and the boxes and the paper towels and all that will fill up a cart pretty quick, so I think I went through everything. There was some produce and that was about it.

INTERVIEWER: Was the list done? Did you guys check everything off?

WALKER: Yeah, and like any Costco trip, there were some things we bought that weren't on that list too.

INTERVIEWER: Give me an example of that.

WALKER: I think some salad and some meat for dinner.

INTERVIEWER: OK, nothing else?

WALKER: Surprisingly no. Maybe a box of . . . actually no, there *was*. There was that box that I insisted on getting because I took something from the "drug dealer" [*Costco's famous free sample "pushers"*], which was the forty-five packages of instant, Eggo mini-pancakes, that now have maple syrup infused in them.

INTERVIEWER: OK. You're getting to the end of this trip.

WALKER: And it's getting stressful. It always gets stressful at the end of Costco, because it's like trying to merge into the Kennedy Expressway in rush hour traffic. They've got a thousand products in the store, but they've got four lanes open. It's getting stressful, we're getting near the end. I actually go down an aisle unexpectedly, and the lightbulb goes off, and there's the mattress.

INTERVIEWER: Why did you think you needed a new mattress? First of all, who had the first thought? You? Your wife?

WALKER: Definitely me first, because about four years prior, I did a lot of research and bought an overpriced Stearns

& Foster that was guaranteed to give me a great night's sleep, and you're going to have a mattress for at least ten years, so it's worth the bigger investment, and we got the cushy pillow top.

I would say for about a year I kept waking up every morning saying, "This bed is awful, I wake up with a headache, a neck ache, and a backache. It's starting to sink, this was a waste of $2,000, I need to find something different."

INTERVIEWER: How long did you enjoy the mattress?

WALKER: Yeah, right when I got it, it was something that I enjoyed for about two years. Year three kind of "eh," year four, couldn't stand it. Had total buyer's remorse.

INTERVIEWER: When did you start to say it was the mattress?

WALKER: Because the backaches and the shoulder and neck aches were always there when waking up that next morning. I tried sleeping without pillows, I tried adjusting my position, all this stuff. As you guys can see I'm not a big, big guy, but I started to notice in the mattress the sinkage.

It felt like I was constantly in this arch, and I woke up every morning thinking, "I don't just need Red Bull, I need three Advil or something else."

INTERVIEWER: You suggest you travel a lot?

WALKER: Last year I did.

INTERVIEWER: OK, and did you not have these problems when you were on the road?

WALKER: I did not. Last year was the first year of my business, and I was gone thirty-seven weeks. I was holed up in the Marriott Renaissance Center three days a week. I would assure you at least that that mattress was not the one that I had at home, but I didn't have those problems.

INTERVIEWER: What else did you do? Did you change anything about the mattress at home? You said you tried no pillows.

WALKER: Yeah, I flipped it, I rotated it, I turned it upside down, I took it off the frame, took it off the box springs.

INTERVIEWER: Was your wife having a problem sleeping?

WALKER: It's funny, because she started, I would say the last six months, to realize too, whether it was guilt by association or legitimate, she would say, "I'm starting to have problems, too. It's uncomfortable," and believe me, as I said, I'm not a big guy and she's probably half of me.

She was saying, "I'm having the same problems, and you can see it's starting to sink, and this pillow top isn't what I thought it was going to be." And by the way, I feel bad because it was my uncle who sold it to me!

INTERVIEWER: Were you complaining to your wife about this? Were you complaining about the condition you were in, or was this something you felt internally?

WALKER: Initially, I felt it, and then I started voicing it. Then she started saying, "Why are you so cranky?"

INTERVIEWER: Do you remember when she actually first told you that she was being affected by it? Do you remember that conversation, or when it was approximately?

WALKER: I would say it's probably about six months ago.

INTERVIEWER: You're on the road all the time, and you're cranky, you need to come home, you've got two kids. When did that argument happen? It had to be something like OK, you come home and you're cranky but I'm not sleeping, so there had to be some conflict around that discussion at some point in time.

WALKER: Yeah, and "Hey, you've been gone all week, so you can be a dad for three days."

INTERVIEWER: Why didn't you go get a new mattress earlier? It sounded like you knew it for a year. Why did you wait so long to get a mattress?

WALKER: I think life gets in the way, between building a

company over the last eighteen months and trying to raise two kids in a small condo and sell it, and then move to a different place. Buying a new mattress was not top of my priority list.

INTERVIEWER: When did you move?

WALKER: June.

INTERVIEWER: You brought the old mattress with you?

WALKER: I had bought my original mattress at Macy's Home Store. Yeah, well, the other caveat that makes this interesting that you might have heard me say, it was sold to me by my uncle.

INTERVIEWER: Had you done a lot of research before you bought that mattress?

WALKER: Yes, I did. I was hoping that my uncle would actually give me a deal, which I found out at checkout he wasn't going to. When my problems started to occur, I went back to Macy's Home Store and asked some questions, "Well, you've got to rotate your mattress. Well, you've got to try this. Well, is it maybe how you're sleeping? Well, our warranty is good for this, but it covers sinkage, and what you have to do is lay a yardstick across the sink of the mattress."

INTERVIEWER: Did you do that?

WALKER: I did not do that, because they said it had to be at least an inch and a half. Then I thought in my head, and other people suggested, "Why don't you get some giant bags of cement and set it in where the sinkholes are already, and have the guy come out and measure the holes?"

INTERVIEWER: Who suggested the cement bags?

WALKER: As I had said earlier on that although there's these little sink areas on each side of the bed, it didn't get an inch and a half. The warranty didn't matter, so I wasn't going to get any recourse there.

INTERVIEWER: At some point you're not sleeping well. You're all stressed. You're in the middle of Costco, taking a shortcut to try to ease your way onto the Kennedy a little bit faster, get out of there faster, and you see a mattress. You say, "This is the time." What made you think you had the time today to get that? Because you had to go all the way back and get a flatbed and reenter the Kennedy to get out.

WALKER: As we talked about, this is mid-September. Now let's rewind about three months. Within that three-month window, I started doing research, saying, "The old mattress has to be replaced." The idea of going into a mattress store or furniture store just gave me the skeeves. I did a lot of online research, and I thought, "You know what? I'm going to make a commitment to a memory foam mattress of some kind."

I did a lot of online research, came this close to pulling the trigger on a Groupon for a memory foam mattress, and said after my experience with Macy's Home Store, the last thing I want to do is order something through Groupon online. In the event that I don't like it, then what am I going to do?

Then this brings us back to the day of, apparently, the crime and the crime scene. I'm in the aisle, and all of a sudden here are all these different memory foam mattresses. I'm like, OK. I'm in Costco. I've done a lot of research. The idea of box springs versus eighteen-inch versus twelve versus coils, none of that stuff had ever even gone through my head.

To me, it was about a good night's sleep. Waking up, feeling pretty good, so I could be as productive as I could be as a business guy and a dad and a husband the next day. I see this, my kids are talking about how they want to get pizza in the checkout, and I'm like OK. Here it is.

I had to go back for the flatbed because I'm like, I pull it down and realize, this is really heavy. The biggest thing that fascinated me is if anyone has bought one of these is to know actually how to package. Because it's in a box about this high, about that wide, cube rectangle I guess. I'm like, "Wow."

As you had asked me, the cart was pretty full. Trying to throw that on top of everything else wasn't going to work.

INTERVIEWER: What was your wife doing at the time? Was your wife going, "Good idea," was she going, "Oh, come on"?

WALKER: She was a little skeptical. She was probably more content in keeping my kids from hitting each other. There was some franticness. There was some, "Are you sure you want it?" Then I pulled down the little twelve-inch by twelve-inch sample of the foam. "Here touch it, feel it."

"Oh, that's actually not bad. If you want it, get it. It's not a lot of money, I know you're not sleeping, get it." That's when I went out and got the flatbed.

INTERVIEWER: How much was it? Do you remember what you paid?

WALKER: Yeah, it was $699. It's funny, because the Groupon happens to be available, and the one on Groupon was less, but again I felt very concerned about if I have a bad experience about this, do I want to go the Groupon online route versus getting it at the Costco that's five minutes from my house?

INTERVIEWER: Was there one kind of mattress or was there a huge assortment?

WALKER: Not a huge assortment, but there were two or three different kinds, and then they had them by your different bed sizes.

INTERVIEWER: Did you squeeze all of them, or?

WALKER: There were two that we were specifically looking at, and one was a lot higher and seemed a lot softer. That was the one that we went with.

INTERVIEWER: Was it the most expensive one?

WALKER: It was.

INTERVIEWER: You had a Groupon, right? What was the store you were going to buy that from? You're not buying it from Groupon. Groupon's offering the promotion. Who was the company that was selling the mattress?

WALKER: I honestly can't think of it now.

INTERVIEWER: The other thing we need to dive into is you made the comment that going into a mattress store gave you the heebie-jeebies, something like that. When's the last time you were in a mattress store, do you remember?

WALKER: I walk by them. I just walked by one the other day.

INTERVIEWER: What happens in a mattress store?

WALKER: First of all, I'm a germaphobe. I see all these beds lined up everywhere and it's creepy. Secondly, I never see someone that is working in the mattress store that has asked anywhere near the level of questions that you've asked me. It's usually a "What size bed do you have? How much are you looking to spend?"

I think there's a lot of people at that mattress world from my previous experiences in them that are the same as the bad notion of the car salesman. I'm not saying they're all that way, it's just that's how some of my experiences have been.

INTERVIEWER: The normal purchase process is impossible for you. You can't walk into a mattress store and even feel it, because there's this anxiety around, you're going to get approached by this salesperson. You never lay on the mattress, I can't believe it.

End of interview

What we see in this interview are the masses of emotion and anxiety this customer has built up around the decision to buy a new mattress. He might be flagged as an impulse buyer at Costco—and marketing decisions might be made around the idea that people buy mattresses on impulse. But the fact is this guy has been thinking about it for a year. It's been weighing on his mind for a long time. Costco may seem the least likely place for him to pull the trigger on the Big Hire—he's in a warehouse store where you can buy socks by the dozen and giant shrimp platters. He's surrounded by noise, and large shopping carts, and employees pushing free food samples. *This* was the place and the moment that he finally decided to buy a new mattress after months of struggle?

Whatever was driving him, it wasn't truly an impulse. And it had nothing to do with the details of the mattress itself. Is he worried about springs? Is he worried about the coils? There's just not a thought of that. He hasn't mentioned anything about the mattress itself yet. Not one detail.

The progress he was trying to make was to get a good night's sleep to be a better husband and father when the rest of his life is taking a toll on him. Something he was desperate to do. Every day that he was forced to make a Little Hire of his old mattress drove him closer and closer to that moment in Costco—in fact, the failed Little Hire moments may have played the most significant role in his decision that day. He wasn't hiring the new mattress as much as he was desperate to fire the old one. That day, in Costco, it was finally time.

There were barriers preventing him from making a choice until that moment. Depending on the job, sometimes the barriers are most profound for the Big Hire. *What gets in the way of someone choosing to make the decision to hire something to solve their job?* But in other cases, the barriers are surrounding the Little Hire. *Why is this solution difficult for you to use—or not, in reality, solving your problem at all?* In both cases, those barriers can be so significant as to cause a consumer to not hire your product in the first place or fire it once they've brought it into their lives. Innovators have to have a heat-seeking sensor for the tensions, struggles, stress, and anxiety of both the Big Hire and the Little Hire. When we go out in search of innovation opportunities we are like detectives trying to piece together a complicated story with all its emotional richness, because only by constructing the *story* can we innovate in ways that change the ending.

The other thing to realize is that this is a minidocumentary with more than one character. His wife is with him in the store and she has to sleep on the bed, too. It might be impossible to make a purchase like that on the spot without your wife because of the anxiety of your spouse criticizing your choice: "You bought this cruddy mattress without consulting me!" Because the consumer and his wife were both in the same place, at the same time, and they could both at least touch it, he was able to alleviate the concern that she'd grumble at the decision he made after the fact. As soon as she said, "OK, I know you're not sleeping well," she gave her blessing. One major anxiety has been removed. And then, knowing that Costco will take it back without fuss, that's the final obstacle. As incredible as it seems, because of the competing forces pushing and pulling his decision, it was easier for him to take that leap, never having lay on it, than it is to walk into the mattress store and lie down.

ADVIL, RED BULL, OR A NEW MATTRESS?

What should a mattress manufacturer or retailer take away from this interview? Given that it is just a single interview—not too much—uncovering jobs is about clustering insights, not having a single eureka. But we can start to form hypotheses and ask fresh questions, as well as think about what we might probe on subsequent interviews.

There's clearly tension around the mattress retailer experience.

What might the ideal experience be for the shopper? Perhaps our salespeople are largely focused on mattress features and the deal. Should we think about staffing our stores with "sleep" experts rather than mattress experts—and might doing so highlight opportunities to improve hiring, training, and compensation structure? When couples will be using a mattress, so both opinions matter, how do you handle the situation where only one spouse is in the store? Should you engage with couples differently? Could you partner with local movers to offer a deal bundled with their move?

There's also anxiety about switching: *What if I don't like the new one? How do I get rid of the old one? To be honest, I really do not want to leave our ten-year-old mattress out by the curb for all the neighbors to view . . . I'm not OK with that.* And the list continues, but you can see how further interviews would lead to additional hypotheses and perhaps the retailer discovers opportunities to include immediate delivery and free mattress removal. Perhaps there's a ninety-day free trial period, no questions asked.

For a mattress manufacturer, one of the big eye-openers might be how dependent we are on the in-store experience and that, if all we think about is our product performance, we're likely missing the real issue. How can we make retailers more successful? How can we and our retail partners adjust our advertising to communicate the benefits that actually will drive store visits and sales? Manufacturers would certainly have considered the traditional set of competitors, but had they considered Advil or Red Bull? In the case of this interviewee, some of his behaviors to compensate for poor sleep involved workarounds such as those. If I were a mattress manufacturer, I would want to have a full understanding of these "competitors" and explore ways to decrease the friction associated with adopting my solution with the promise of consistent, high-quality sleep.

As a nonexpert in the world of mattresses, I am struck by the incredible emotional depth associated with making the decision about the mattress purchase. I'd also never thought much about all the pain points and friction associated with *switching* a mattress—from disposing of the old one to getting the new one home. And then the anxiety of *"What if it's not right or my spouse doesn't like it?"* One of the fundamental mistakes that many marketers make is to collect a handful of data points from a huge sample of respondents when what they really need—and this interview illustrates—is a huge number of data points from a smaller sample size. Great innovation insights have more to do with depth than breadth.

"ALL OF A SUDDEN YOU CAN SEE THE PATH . . ."

As many of the executives we interviewed have told us, when you hit upon a job, it just makes intuitive sense. It *feels* true. A genuine insight, as neuromarketing expert Gerald Zaltman, a colleague at Harvard Business School, says, is a thought that is experienced as true on conception. When you have an insight, you don't have to convince yourself that it's important or powerful. You just know.

The key to getting hired is to understand the narrative of the customer's life in such rich detail that you are able to design a solution that far exceeds anything the customer themselves could have found words to request. In hindsight, breakthrough insights might seem obvious, but they rarely are. In fact, they're fundamentally contrarian: you see something that others have missed.

But as our next chapter will illustrate, uncovering a Job to Be Done is only the first step. You are selling progress, not products. In order to create a solution that customers actually want to hire—and hire repeatedly—you have to see the full context of customers' Jobs to Be Done and the obstacles that get in their way.

- Deeply understanding a customer's real Job to Be Done can be challenging in practice. Customers are often unable to articulate what they want; even when they do describe what they want, their actions often tell a completely different story.

- Seemingly objective data about customer behavior is often misleading, as it focuses exclusively on the Big Hire (when the customer actually buys a product) and neglects the Little Hire (when the customer actually uses it). The Big Hire might suggest that a product has solved a customer's job, but only a consistent series of Little Hires can confirm it.

- Before a customer hires any new product, you have to understand what he'll need to fire in order to hire yours. Companies don't think about this enough. Something always needs to get fired.

- Hearing what a customer can't say requires careful observation of and interactions with customers, all carried out while maintaining a "beginner's mind." This mindset helps you to avoid ingoing assumptions that could prematurely filter out critical information.

- Developing a full understanding of the job can be done by assembling a kind of storyboard that describes in rich detail the customer's circumstances, moments of struggle, imperfect experiences, and corresponding frustrations.

- As part of your storyboard, it's critically important to understand the forces that compel change to a new solution, including the "push" of the unsatisfied job itself and the "pull" of the new solution.

- It is also critical to understand the forces opposing any change, including the inertia caused by current habits and the anxiety about the new.

- If the forces opposing change are strong, you can often innovate the experiences you provide in a way that mitigates them, for example by creating experiences that minimize the anxiety of moving to something new.

- What evidence do you have that you've clearly understood your customers' jobs? Do your customers' actions correspond to what they tell you they want? Do you have evidence that your customers make the Little Hire and the Big Hire?
- Can you tell a complete story about how your customers go from a circumstance of struggle, to firing their current solution, and ultimately hiring yours (both the Big and the Little Hires)? Where are there gaps in your storyboard and how can you fill them in?
- What are the forces that impede potential customers from hiring your product? How could you innovate the experiences surrounding your product to overcome these forces?

NOTES

1. Kahneman, Daniel, and Amos Tversky. "Prospect Theory: An Analysis of Decision under Risk." *Econometrica* 47, no. 2, March 1979: 263–92.

2. You can listen to the original, unedited mattress interview on Bob Moesta's website: Jobstobedone.org.

3. It is worth noting how our Theory of Jobs relates to another popular idea related to customer-centric innovation, that of "design thinking." This label is commonly applied to a broad set of ideas and practices, but at its heart it refers to a problem-solving methodology that emphasizes deep empathy with the customer, divergent thinking, and rapid iteration of solutions. A central element of design thinking is to prioritize users' experiences over product attributes, and on this important point we find common ground. Because Jobs Theory provides a *causal* explanation for why customers will embrace some innovations and not others, as well as a language for understanding deeply the insights about customers that really matter, it is complementary to, and completely compatible with, design thinking. The language and thought process of jobs provides a powerful set of tools for developing the deep customer insights required by design thinking, and for inspiring solutions that customers will actually want to purchase and use.

CHAPTER 6

Building Your Résumé

THE BIG IDEA

Uncovering a job in all its rich complexity is only the beginning. You're a long way from getting hired. But truly understanding a Job to Be Done provides a sort of decoder to that complexity—a language that enables clear specifications for solving Jobs to Be Done. New products succeed not because of the features and functionality they offer but because of the experiences they enable.

If you don't have a preteen girl in your life, you may not understand how anyone can consider paying more than a hundred dollars for a doll. But I've done it. Multiple times. That doesn't even count what we've spent on extra clothing and accessories. I think it would have been cheaper for me to buy clothing for myself. My daughter Katie, and many of her friends, coveted pricey American Girl dolls when they were growing up. Check out Craigslist ads right after the holidays—you'll find a shocking number of parents eager to purchase secondhand or homemade American Girl clothing to supplement their daughter's Christmas present. By one estimate, the typical American Girl Doll purchaser will spend more than six hundred dollars in total. To date, the company has sold 29 million dolls and racks up more than $500 million in sales annually.

What's so special about an American Girl doll? Well, it's not the doll itself. They come in a variety of styles and ethnicities and they're lovely, sturdy dolls. But to my eye, they look similar to dolls that children have played with for generations. American Girl dolls are *nice*. But they aren't *amazing*.

In recent years Toys"R"Us, Walmart, and even Disney have all tried to challenge American Girl's success with similar dolls (Journey Girls, My Life, and Princess & Me)—at a fraction of the price—but to date, no one has made a dent. American Girl is able to command a premium price because it's not really selling dolls. It's selling an *experience*.

When you see a company that has a product or service that no one has successfully copied, like American Girl, rarely is it the product itself that is the source of the long-term competitive advantage, something American Girl founder Pleasant Rowland understood. "You're not trying to just get the product out there, you hope you are creating an experience that will do the job perfectly," says Rowland. You're creating experiences that, in effect, make up the product's résumé: *"Here's why you should hire me."*

That's why American Girl has been so successful for so long, in spite of numerous attempts by competitors to elbow in. My wife, Christine, and I were willing to splurge on the dolls because we understood what they stood for. American Girl dolls are about connection and empowering self-belief—and the chance to savor childhood just a bit longer. I have found that creating the right set of experiences around a clearly defined job—and then organizing the company around delivering those experiences (which we'll discuss in the next chapter)—almost inoculates you against disruption. Disruptive competitors almost never come with a better sense of the job. They don't see beyond the product. Preteen girls hire the dolls to help articulate their feelings and validate who they are—their identities, their sense of self, and their cultural and racial background—and offer them hope that they can surmount the challenges in their lives. The Job to Be Done for *parents,* who are actually purchasing the doll, is to help engage both mothers and daughters in a rich conversation about the generations of women that came before them, and their struggles and their strength. Those conversations had disappeared as more and more women entered the workforce in the years after the women's movement, and mothers and grandmothers were craving an opportunity to bring them back into their lives.

"There's no question in my mind that I came from the thesis that innovation succeeds when it addresses a job that needs to be done," says Rowland, whose unsatisfactory options while shopping for a Christmas present for her nieces triggered the idea. At the time, the most popular options were either hypersexualized Barbies or Cabbage Patch Kids, neither of which would help her connect with her beloved nieces. Her vision for the company, which was born almost entirely out of her own childhood memories, was built around creating similar happy experiences for the mothers and daughters who buy American Girl dolls. As I said in chapter 4, our lives are very articulate.

The dolls—and their worlds—reflect Rowland's nuanced and sophisticated understanding of the job. There are dozens of American Girl dolls representing a broad cross section of profiles. For example, there's Kaya, a young girl from a Northwest Native American tribe in the late eighteenth century. Her back story tells of her leadership, her compassion, her courage, and her loyalty. There's Kristen Larson, a Swedish immigrant who settles in the Minnesota territory and faces hardships and challenges but triumphs in the end. There's modern-era Lindsey Bergman who is focused on her upcoming bat mitzvah. And so on. A significant part of the allure is the well-written, historically accurate books about each character's life that express feelings and struggles that the preteen owner might be sharing. The books may be even more popular than the dolls themselves.

Rowland and her team thought through every aspect of the experience required to perform the job very, very well. The dolls were never sold in traditional toy stores, thrown in the mix alongside any number of competitors. They were initially available only through a catalog, then later at American Girl stores, which were initially created in a few major metropolitan areas. It turned out this added to the experience, turning a trip to the American Girl store into a special day out with mom (or dad). American Girl stores have doll hospitals that can repair tangled hair or fix broken parts. Some of the stores have restaurants in which parents, children, and their dolls can happily sit and be served from a kid-friendly menu—or host birthday parties. The dolls become the catalyst for experiences with mom and dad that will be remembered forever.

No detail was too small to consider for its experiential value. That familiar red-and-pink packaging that the dolls come in? Rowland designed them with a clear window of the doll inside, but they were wrapped with what's known as a belly band—a narrow wrapper around the whole box—and the dolls were packed in tissue paper. That belly band, Rowland remembers, added two cents and twenty-seven seconds to the actual packaging process itself. The designers suggested they simply print the doll's name right on the box itself to save time and money—an idea Rowland rejected out of hand. "I said you're not getting it. What has to happen to make this special to the child? I don't want her to see some shrink-wrapped thing coming out of the box. The fact that she has to wait just a split second to get the band off and open the tissue under the lid makes it exciting to open the box. It's not the same as walking down the aisle in the toy store and picking a Barbie off the shelf. That's the kind of detail we tended to. I just kept going back to my own childhood to the things that made me excited."

American Girl was so successful in nailing the Job to Be Done of both mothers and daughters that it was able to use its core offerings—and the loyalty they established—as a platform to expand into what might seem to be wildly diverse fields. Dolls, books, retail stores, movies, clothes, restaurants, beauty parlors, and even a live theater in Chicago, all of which Rowland actually had in mind before she launched the company. They simply made intuitive sense to her—based on the happy experiences of her own childhood—and aligned squarely with the job. Going to the live theater for an American Girl show? That harkened back to the days when she used to put on white gloves to go to Chicago Symphony concerts with her own mother. "That was a moment I was trying to re-create for girls when they went to the American Girl store. It was very much coming out of my life experience," she explains. "I simply trusted my memories of childhood."

Three decades after its launch, there's a generation of American Girl fans who are now adults and eager to share the dolls—and the experiences they enable—with their own children. We have a family friend who still buys American Girl dolls for her adult daughter at Christmas with the express wish that she hands them down to her own daughters someday.

Under Mattel's ownership, it has seen a slight dip in sales in the past couple of years, but no one has been successful in unseating American Girl from its perch. "I think nobody was willing to put the depth in the product to create the experience," says Rowland. "They thought it was a product. They never got the story part right." To date, no other toy manufacturer has been able to copy American Girl's magic formula.

DECODING THE COMPLEXITY

As I've discussed, jobs are complex and multifaceted. But a deep understanding of a job provides a sort of decoder to the complexity—a job spec, if you will. Whereas the job itself is the framing of the circumstance from the perspective of the consumer with the Job to Be Done, as he or she confronts a struggle to make progress, the *job spec* is from the innovator's point of view: *What do I need to design, develop, and deliver in my new product offering so that it solves the consumer's job well?* You can capture the relevant details of the job in a job spec, including the functional, emotional, and social dimensions that define the desired progress, the tradeoffs the customer is willing to make, the full set of competing solutions that must be beaten, and the obstacles and anxieties that must be overcome. That understanding should then be matched by an offering that includes a plan to surmount the obstacles and create the right set of experiences in purchasing and using the product. The job spec then becomes the blueprint that translates all the richness and complexity of the job into an actionable guide for innovation. Designed without a clear job spec, even the most advanced products are likely to fail. There are just too many details to nail and tricky tradeoffs to be made in creating customer value for innovators to rely on the luck of just guessing right. The experiences you create to respond to the job spec are critical to creating a solution that customers not only want to hire, but want to hire over and over again. There's a reason successful jobs-based innovations are hard to copy—it's in this level of detail that organizations create long-term competitive advantage because this is how customers decide what products are better than other products.

EXPERIENCES AND PREMIUM PRICES

In my classroom I share an illustration with my students to highlight how to think about innovating around jobs. It's just a simple representation, but it's intended to underscore the point that although identifying and understanding the Job to Be Done is the foundation, it's only the first step in creating products that you can be sure customers want to hire. Products that they'll actually *pay premium prices* for.

That involves not only understanding the job, but also the right set of experiences for purchase and use of that product, and then integrating those experiences into a company's processes. All three layers—Uncovering the Job, Creating the Desired Experiences, and Integrating around the Job—are critical. When a company understands and responds to all three layers of the job depicted here, it will have solved a job in a way that competitors can't easily copy.

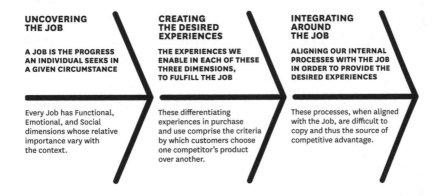

UNCOVERING THE JOB

A JOB IS THE PROGRESS AN INDIVIDUAL SEEKS IN A GIVEN CIRCUMSTANCE

Every Job has Functional, Emotional, and Social dimensions whose relative importance vary with the context.

CREATING THE DESIRED EXPERIENCES

THE EXPERIENCES WE ENABLE IN EACH OF THESE THREE DIMENSIONS, TO FULFILL THE JOB

These differentiating experiences in purchase and use comprise the criteria by which customers choose one competitor's product over another.

INTEGRATING AROUND THE JOB

ALIGNING OUR INTERNAL PROCESSES WITH THE JOB IN ORDER TO PROVIDE THE DESIRED EXPERIENCES

These processes, when aligned with the Job, are difficult to copy and thus the source of competitive advantage.

© JAMES DE VRIES

Consider IKEA, for example. IKEA is one of the most profitable companies in the world and has been so for decades. Its owner, Ingvar Kamprad, is one of the wealthiest men in the world. How did he make so much money selling nondescript furniture that you have to assemble yourself? He identified a Job to Be Done.

Here's a business that doesn't have any special business secrets. Any would-be competitor can walk through its stores, reverse-engineer its products, or copy its catalog. But no one has. Why not? IKEA's entire business model—the shopping experience, the layout of the store, the design of the products and the way they are packaged—is very different from the standard furniture store.

Most retailers are organized around a customer segment or a type of product. The customer base can then be divided up into target demographics, such as age, gender, education, or income level. There are competitors who sell to wealthy people—Roche Bobois sells sofas that cost thousands of dollars! There are stores known for selling low-cost furniture to lower-income people. And there are a host of other examples: stores organized around modern furniture for urban dwellers, stores that specialize in furniture for businesses, and so on.

IKEA doesn't focus on selling to any particular demographically defined group of consumers. IKEA is structured around jobs that lots of consumers share when they are trying to establish themselves and their families in new surroundings: *I've got to get this place furnished tomorrow, because the next day I have to show up at work.*

Other furniture stores can copy IKEA's products. They can even copy IKEA's layout. But what has been difficult to copy are the experiences that IKEA provides its customers—and the way it has anticipated and helped its customers overcome the obstacles that get in their way.

Nobody I know relishes the idea of spending a day shopping for furniture when they really, really need it right away. It's not entertainment, it's a frustrating challenge. Factor in that your children will likely be with you when you're shopping and it could be a recipe for disaster. IKEA stores have a designated child-care area where you can leave your children to play while you wind your way through the store—and a café and ice cream stand to offer as a reward at the end. Don't want to wait to get your bookshelves home? They're flat-packed in cartons that can fit in or on most cars. Is it daunting to lay out all the parts to an unbuilt bookshelf and then have to put it together yourself? Absolutely. But it's not overwhelming because IKEA has designed all its products to require just one simple tool (that's included with every flat pack—

· and actually stored inside one of the pieces of wood so you can't accidentally lose it when you open the box!). And everyone I know who has tackled an IKEA assembly ends up feeling pretty proud of himself or herself when it's done.

Who is IKEA competing with? My son Michael hired it when he moved to California to start his doctoral studies: *"Help me furnish my place* today." He's got to decide what he'll hire to do the job. So how does he decide? He has to have some kind of criteria to make his choice. At a fundamental level, he will factor in how much he cares about the basics of the offering: cost and quality, and the priorities and tradeoffs he's willing to make in the context of the job he needs to get done. But he'll care even more about what experiences each possible solution offers him in solving his job. And what obstacles he'd have to overcome to hire each possible solution.

He'll hire IKEA, even if it costs more than some of those other solutions, because it does the job better than any alternatives. The reason why we are willing to pay *premium prices* for a product that nails the job is because the *full cost* of a product that fails to do the job—wasted time, frustration, spending money on poor solutions, and so on—is significant to us. The "struggle" is costly—you're already spending time and energy to find a solution and so, even when a premium price comes along, your internal calculus makes that look small compared with what you've already been spending, not only financially, but also in personal resources.

Other furniture stores might offer Michael free delivery, but it will probably take days or even weeks to deliver the furniture he wants to purchase. What is he going to sit on tomorrow? Craigslist offers bargains, but he'll have to cobble together his furniture choices and rent a car to drive all over town to get them, probably enlisting a friend to help him lug them up and down the stairs. Discount furniture stores might offer some of IKEA's benefits, but they're not likely to be so easy to assemble at home. Unfinished furniture stores have decent quality products, but you have to paint them yourself! That's not easy to pull off in a small apartment. He's not likely to feel good about any of these other choices.

You can only shape the experiences that are important to your customers when you understand who you are really competing with. That's how you'll know how to create your résumé to be hired for the job. And when you get that all right, your customers will be more than willing to pay a premium price because you'll solve their job better than anyone else.

I should clarify, however: sometimes customers get pushed into paying for premium products because they're interdependent with a product that they have already hired to solve a job in their lives. Think about the eye-popping price tag for printer-ink cartridges. Or smartphone rechargers or cases. We'll give in and pay the premium price because there isn't a better solution at the moment, but we will simultaneously despise the company for taking us to the cleaners. These products actually *cause* anxiety, rather than resolve it. I hated having to monitor how much color ink my kids were using on our home printer. I don't like worrying about misplacing a charger. This is *not* what I mean about premium prices that customers are willing to pay. By contrast, with jobs-based innovations, customers don't resent the price, they're grateful for the solution.

REMOVING THE OBSTACLES

Products that succeed in solving customers' jobs essentially perform services in that customer's life. They help them overcome the obstacles that get in their way of making the progress they seek. *"Help me furnish this apartment today." "Help me share our rich family history with my child."* Creating experiences and overcoming obstacles is how a product becomes a *service* to the customer, rather than simply a product with better features and benefits.

Medical-device manufacturer Medtronic learned this the hard way when it was trying to introduce a new pacemaker in India.

On the surface, it seemed like a market full of potential, because, unfortunately, heart disease is the country's number one killer. But for a variety of reasons, very few patients ever ended up opting for a pacemaker to solve their medical problem. For years, Medtronic had relied on traditional forms of research to develop its product offerings. "We were very good at understanding *functional* jobs," recalls Keyne Monson, then senior director of international business development at the medical device manufacturer. For example, when Medtronic was looking to improve its pacemakers, it assembled panels of doctors to pick their brains about what they'd like to see in the next generation of the devices. The company then fielded quantitative surveys that validated the physician panels' feedback and new products were created.

The new versions of Medtronic's pacemaker were clearly superior, but unfortunately they didn't sell in India as well as the company had hoped. It had been nagging at Monson for some time that neither the qualitative nor quantitative approaches Medtronic had historically relied on had actually answered the question of *why* people would want to hire a pacemaker and what obstacles might get in their way—and to do so for the broader set of stakeholders involved.

With the lens of Jobs to Be Done, the Medtronic team and Innosight (including my coauthor David Duncan) started research afresh in India. The team visited hospitals and care facilities, interviewing more than a hundred physicians, nurses, hospital administrators, and patients across the country. The research turned up four key barriers preventing patients from receiving much-needed cardiac care:

Lack of patient awareness of health and medical needs
Lack of proper diagnostics
Inability of patients to navigate the care pathway
Affordability

While there were competitors making some progress in India, the biggest competition was nonconsumption because of the challenges the Medtronic team identified.

From a traditional perspective, Medtronic might have doubled down on doctors, asking them about priorities and tradeoffs in the product. What features would they value more, or less? Asking patients what they wanted would not have been top of the list of considerations from a marketing perspective.

But when Medtronic revisited the problem through the lens of Jobs to Be Done, Monson says, the team realized that the picture was far more complex—and not one that Medtronic executives could have figured out from pouring over statistics of Indian heart disease or asking cardiologists how to make the pacemaker better. Medtronic has missed a critical component of the Job to Be Done.

The experience of being a candidate for a pacemaker was filled with stresses and obstacles. For a patient to receive a pacemaker to help solve his heart issues, he would have had to navigate a complicated path. First, he might have seen a local general practitioner (GP), typically the first line of medical care, but not always someone with formal medical training. Each of these doctors saw hundreds of patients in a given day. "There were patient lines stretching down the hall," Monson recalls. "There were so many people waiting to see the local GP, they actually pushed from the hallway into the doctor's interview room and were lining the walls there, too." The local GP had about thirty seconds with each patient and then he was passed on, either with a prescription, recommendations, or a referral to a specialist. Symptoms that might suggest a pacemaker can be easily confused with those of other medical conditions. It would be virtually impossible for a prospective patient to find his way from a brief GP visit to the right heart surgeon to implant a pacemaker.

Even if he did get that far, referral to a higher-order specialist meant the patient was jettisoned into a system in which he was a complete stranger to the medical teams who would take the process further. Navigating the referral process after a GP did recommend someone for a pacemaker was confusing—and expensive—for a patient who had to pay for health care out of pocket.

So Medtronic adjusted not only its marketing efforts, but also the services it provided to directly target potential patients. For example, in conjunction with local cardiologists, Medtronic organized heart-health screening clinics across the country—providing prospective patients with free, direct access to specialists and high-tech equipment without having to go through an overwhelmed GP first.

The question of paying for a pacemaker and the attendant medical services was no small concern. So Medtronic created a loan program to help patients pay for the pacemaker procedure. The company initially assumed that patients might be drawn to loans that actually expired upon the patient's death, so that they were not saddling the family with the burden of debt—the emotional and social component of their Job to Be Done. And, as the Medtronic team learned from patients themselves, that was what they often wanted. But friends and family wanted something different: they tended to rally around a patient to find the money necessary. In those cases, the patient was more likely simply to need a bridge loan until those funds could be gathered. Medtronic made sure that the loan process was not daunting for the family: a loan is typically approved within two days, requiring minimum paperwork and entailing no asset mortgage.

The experience of navigating the complex web of health care in India could be overwhelming for both patients and their families. So the company began to work with local hospitals to create a patient counselor role, initially calling them "Sherpas," that helped patients navigate the often mind-boggling bureaucracy of a hospital, keeping their procedure and aftercare as top priorities.

The patient counselor role became so popular that hospitals asked if the company would allow patients obtaining pacemakers through traditional routes to seek assistance from a counselor, too. Seeing an opportunity to further identify Jobs to Be Done from within the hospital system, Medtronic jumped at the chance. "At the end of the day, we realized the role was such an important position, we adjusted the role. And we were OK with it," Monson recalls. "It ingrained the value of that person into the entire hospital system, and thus our business model. And it made us the partner of choice. To me that was a clear example of hitting a Job to Be Done."

The first Medtronic pacemaker distributed through the Healthy Heart for All (HHFA) program in India was implanted in late 2010. Medtronic currently has partnerships with more than one hundred hospitals in thirty cities. India is considered to be one of the most high-potential growth markets for the company.

According to Shamik Dasgupta, vice president of the Cardiac and Vascular Group, Indian Sub-Continent, Medtronic, "Under the HHFA initiative since its beginning till December 2015, around 167,000 patients have undergone screenings for heart diseases till date, out of which 89,900 patients were counselled and around 15,000 patients have received treatment, with financial assistance facility availed in approximately 550 cases."

Making that possible involved creating relationships with several partners who helped Medtronic accomplish customers' jobs. "Through the assessment of Healthy Heart for All, Medtronic understood the need for partners in different stages of the patient care pathway who can be a strong support in removing the barriers to treatment access," says Dasgupta. "In this case, partners with capabilities in financing, administration of loans, screening and counselling of patients played a major role. With programs like Healthy Heart for All, Medtronic is delivering greater value to patients, healthcare professionals and hospitals. And it is this value which brings true differentiation where product differentiation may not be easy to demonstrate."

THE UBER EXPERIENCE

The value of creating the right set of experiences in a circumstance-specific job is clearly not universally understood. I don't know anyone who relishes the experience of renting a car, for example. You land at an airport, tired from travel, and eager to get on the road to your destination. But first you have to find your particular car rental counter in the arrivals area of the airport or figure out where you can find the shuttle bus to take you to a large parking lot offsite where your car will be waiting for you. The lines to check in or check out are often long, and it's not uncommon to finally get to the front of the line and learn you could have done some form of "speedy check-in" instead. You have to time your return of the car rental to allow you to fill up the gas tank right before you turn into the lot because you don't want to have to pay above-market rates for a top-up. And every renter I know anxiously hovers around the person checking the car back in to make sure you're not later held responsible for scratches or dings that the car rental company declares happened on your watch. Some car-rental locations close early on the weekends, impacting your decision about when you need to get back to the airport. Even when nothing goes wrong, it's almost always an unpleasant experience, with attendant frustrations and anxieties.

Simply Google "car rental reviews" and you'll see how much customers love the experience of renting a car. It's not hard to find hashtags that tell us how well the car-rental industry is serving its customers: you'll easily find #hertzsucks and #avissucks on Twitter, to name just two. Online you'll find an onslaught of complaints, most mentioning nothing about the cars the companies rent, but focusing instead on the experience that accompanied actually renting the car. Yet with the exception of some minor tinkering at the edge (skip the counter at the airport for frequent customers), car-rental companies continue to compete almost exclusively on price or the variety of cars they have to offer.

Customers actively seek out workarounds—even if they're imperfect. If they're traveling for business and they're senior enough in a company, they might impose on junior local staff to get the rental car and then pick them up at arrivals. Or hire a car service for the full day. I know of one guy who, when his plane was unexpectedly diverted, paid for an Uber all the way from Milwaukee to Chicago rather than endure the stress and hassle of renting a car.

These workarounds should be warning signs to the car-rental industry—which may find itself facing an onslaught from new competitors in the near future as the job of "mobility" takes shape. Failing to deliver the experiences that help your customers solve their Jobs to Be Done leaves you vulnerable to disruption as better solutions come along and customers swiftly jump ship.

By contrast, one company that clearly understands the stakes is Uber. In the last several years, few companies have captured the media's attention like Uber. In my opinion, Uber has been successful because it's perfectly nailed a Job to Be Done. Yes, Uber can often offer a nice car to take you from point A to point B, but that's not where it's built its competitive advantage. The experiences that come with hiring Uber to solve customers' Jobs to Be Done are better than the existing alternatives. *That's* the secret to its success.

Everything about the experience of being a customer—including the emotional and social dimensions—has been thought through. Who wants to have to outmaneuver other poor schlubs on the same street corner who are trying to hail a cab? You don't want to either pay for a car service to wait outside your meeting or be at its mercy when you're finally ready to call it to come back and get you. With Uber, you simply push a few buttons on your mobile phone and you know that in three minutes or seven minutes a specific driver will arrive to pick you up. Now you can relax and just wait. You don't have to worry if you have enough cash in your wallet or fear that if you swipe your credit card in that taxi machine, you'll get a call from your bank wondering if you've recently made purchases in some state you've never even been to. Calling an Uber has even more potential to ease your anxieties about getting into a cab alone. With Uber there's a record of your request, you know specifically who is picking you up, and you know from the driver's ratings that he or she is reliable. Uber isn't just competing with taxis and car services, it's also competing with opting to take the subway home or calling a friend.

Organizations that focus on making the product itself better and better are missing what may be the most powerful causal mechanism of all—*what are the experiences that customers seek in not only purchasing, but also in using this product?* If you don't know the answer to that question, you're probably not going to be hired.

HOW DO I KNOW YOU'RE RIGHT FOR THE JOB?

Amazon, too, knows exactly what experiences its customers value. Everything is built around delivering those experiences well. There are many factors that have enabled Amazon's meteoric growth, but there is no way it could be "the everything store" without its customer reviews. In fact, I'd argue that it's probably the hardest thing for any would-be competitor to copy.

Why are Amazon's reviews so powerful? Because they help customers make the progress they want to make. If I look around my house or my friends' houses, for example, I can see a wide variety of products that were purchased on Amazon. A TV. A rice steamer. A digital camera. A smoothie maker. What enables me and millions of others to buy unfamiliar items with greater confidence by virtue of a listing on a website? The requisite list of features and functionality doesn't help me much—in fact my eye tends to skip right over that section. But it does go immediately to the line that tells me where I can figure out if this is the right product to hire for my job: "56 reviews. 21 answered questions."

Sure, seeing an item with a bunch of four-out-of-five-star ratings helps, but what I really need to know is what do reviewers who were hiring for the same job as me have to say? There might be lots of toaster oven reviews about whether it browns the toast evenly (there are, apparently, a lot of people who care about that stuff!), but I really want to know whether it will help me heat a frozen pizza when I don't want to crank up our conventional oven. I'm sure many people care about the pixels and zoom on a digital camera, but I just want to know that it is easy to set up and use. In other words, Amazon allows me to shop unfamiliar categories with total confidence because I can find folks who share my job and gauge the performance that matters most to me from those reviews.

Amazon clearly understands the importance of these reviews. There are Hall of Fame reviewers (so noted on each review) and top ten thousand reviewer rankings—ranked by the number and percentage of helpful votes their reviews have received. In 2015 Amazon also introduced technology that automates giving more weight to newer reviews, reviews from verified Amazon purchasers, and reviews that more customers voted as being helpful.

Companies that sell their wares on Amazon are so sensitive to the power of these reviews that they routinely email their customers shortly after the purchase has arrived at its destination to ask if they have any feedback—hoping to preempt any negative feedback before they end up on the review page. They go to extraordinary lengths, including no-hassle refunds or replacements, rather than risk a bad review from a top reviewer who will, certainly, influence how many people hire that product for their Job to Be Done. The experience that those reviews provide other customers is highly valued: *"I don't want the hassle of having to return it or just considering it wasted money. And I don't want to wait two days to find out I still need another solution. How can I be sure I'm not making a mistake?"*

Online reviews have fundamentally improved the experience of purchasing almost anything in recent years. We can check reviews on everything from auto repair shops to insurance companies with a few clicks on our keyboard. Online reviews help great products get hired.

But they are a two-sided coin. From the business's perspective, they represent the first time in history where you have to think about how to convey who should *not* hire your product. A customer who hires your product or service for a job it is not intended to do will be sorely disappointed—and perhaps write a disgruntled online review. Negative reviews can break a business. Restaurant owners routinely grouse about being held hostage to their Yelp ratings, at the mercy of reviews by uninformed palates. Airbnb works with its "host" customers to make sure their listings make very clear who should—and shouldn't—hire that particular listing, says Airbnb's Chip Conley. Airbnb advises hosts to imagine that there's "an invisible report card on the forehead of potential guests," rating everything about how the actual location met their expectations. "Overselling" your listing will work against you very quickly on Airbnb—and in the increasing number of marketplaces in which reviews function almost like a currency.

Airbnb listings emphasize what the local neighborhood is like and what kind of experience guests will have in the home. Is it convenient? Is it quiet and peaceful? Is it in the center of action? All those details are important to capture in both the description and photos so that guests won't be disappointed with their choice—and write a poor review.

Research has suggested that as many as 95 percent of consumers use reviews and 86 percent say they are essential when making purchase decisions.[1] And nearly one-third of consumers under the age of forty-five consult reviews for *every single purchase*. Businesses now have to consider how to educate customers about what job these products and services are designed to do[2]—and when potential customers should not consider hiring them. That is a new wrinkle.

PURPOSE BRAND

There is a tool that helps you avoid leaving your product or service vulnerable to customers who hire it for the wrong reasons. Done perfectly, your brand can become synonymous with the job—what's known as a purpose brand. When I list these brands, you will surely instantly know what job they've been hired to do:

Uber
TurboTax
Disney
Mayo Clinic
OnStar
Harvard
Match.com
OpenTable
LinkedIn

And one of my personal favorites, Jack Bauer. When you need to save the world in twenty-four hours, Jack Bauer is your man.

A product that consistently creates the right experiences for resolving customers' jobs should speak to the consumer: *"Your search is over, pick me!"* If you need to furnish the apartment you just rented or outfit your daughter's dorm room, you better hope there's an IKEA nearby. IKEA has become a purpose brand for *"Help me furnish my apartment today."*

Purpose brands play the role of communicating externally how the "enclosed attributes" are designed to deliver a very complete and specific experience. A purpose brand is positioned on the mechanism that *causes* people to purchase a product: they nail the job. A purpose brand tells them to hire you for their job.

The reward for perfectly performing a job is not brand fame or brand love—though that may follow—but rather that customers will weave you into the fabric of their lives. Because purpose brands integrate around important Jobs to Be Done rather than conform to established bases of competition, purpose brands frequently re-configure industry structure, change the basis of competition, and command premium prices.

If you wanted to enjoy a decent single cup of coffee at home, you were in a world of trouble before Keurig came to your rescue. The parental lifesaver known as Lunchables didn't exactly compete with the deli counter, the cheese department, or the cracker aisle, but they sure made life easier. Before Fred Smith launched FedEx, urgent documents had to be handed to couriers who would then fly anywhere to meet an important deadline.

FedEx is now a household name, but breaking into the market might have seemed impossible decades ago. But through a job lens, it makes sense. When competitors successfully enter markets that seem closed and commoditized, they do it by aligning with an important job that none of the established players has prioritized. Pixar gave theatergoers a reason to care about the studio producing a film. The Apple brand assures people that the technology will be easy to use and elegantly designed. American Girl enables mothers and daughters to connect and create shared experiences in ways that defy industry categorization.

Milwaukee Electric Tool Corporation has cornered the market in two areas with its strong purpose brands: Sawzall and HOLE HAWG. Sawzall is a reciprocating saw that tradesmen hire when they need to cut through a wall quickly and aren't sure what's under the surface. It's hired for the job of helping tradesmen saw safely through pretty much anything. No panic required when you start the saw. When I look at a wall and I don't know what's behind it, there's one thought that jumps into my mind: where is my Sawzall?

Plumbers hire Milwaukee's HOLE HAWG, a right-angle drill, when they need to drill a hole in a tight space. Competitors like Black & Decker, Bosch, and Makita offer reciprocating saws and right-angle drills with comparable performance and price, but none of them has a purpose brand that pops into a tradesman's mind when he has one of these jobs to do. Milwaukee has owned more than 80 percent of these two job markets for decades.

The company's other tools, which rely on the Milwaukee brand, are not nearly as celebrated. The word "Milwaukee" doesn't give you any market whatsoever. But Sawzall and HOLE HAWG are hired for very specific jobs—and they've become purpose brands.

Purpose brands provide remarkable clarity. They become synonymous with the job. A well-developed purpose brand will stop a consumer from even considering looking for another option. They want *that* product. The price premium that a purpose brand commands is the wage that customers are willing to pay the brand for providing this guidance.

Federal Express illustrates how successful purpose brands are built. A job had existed practically forever: the *"I need to send this from here to there—as fast as possible with perfect certainty"* job. Some US customers hired the US Postal Service's airmail; a few desperate souls paid couriers to sit on airplanes. But because nobody had yet designed a service to do this job well, the brands of the unsatisfactory alternative services became tarnished when they were hired for this purpose. But after Federal Express specifically designed its service to do that exact job, and did it wonderfully again and again, the FedEx brand began popping into people's minds.

This was not built through advertising. It was built through people hiring the service and finding that it got the job done. FedEx became a purpose brand—in fact, it became a verb in the international language of business that is inextricably linked with that specific job.

A very long list of purpose brands, including Starbucks, Google, and craigslist.org, were actually built with minimal advertising at the outset. They're such strong brands that they've become verbs: "Just Google it." But they have been successful because each is associated with a clear purpose—they've been optimized around a clear Job to Be Done. These brands just pop into consumers' minds when they have a Job to Be Done.

By the same token, brands that fail to integrate around a job risk becoming category placeholders—forced to compete on price, slugging it out with look-alike competitors. Just think airlines, automakers, business hotel chains, rental-car companies, or PC-clone manufacturers. Being called a "clone" can never be a good thing.

But it can be all too easy for an organization to lose its understanding of the power of a purpose brand when it falls into the bad habits of adding new benefits and features in the interest of creating marketplace "news" or justifying a price increase. For years, Volvo was the family car in my hometown. The distinctive, boxy cars were ubiquitous in the parking lots of schools, grocery stores, and baseball fields all across town. They may have cost more than other family car options and, let's face it, they were unattractive—but they stood for something important: safety. As far back as its founding in 1927, its two original leaders set the compass directly on this purpose: "Cars are driven by people. The guiding principle behind everything we make at Volvo, therefore, is and must remain, safety." And in the decades since then, the Swedish car company had earned its sterling reputation—as a purpose brand for safety and reliability.

But after Ford purchased Volvo in 1999, it seemed to veer off that clear brand, creating flashier cars to try to compete with luxury standard vehicles. The result was not only a decline in sales—but an opening in the market for competitors' cars to tout their own safety features. Volvo no longer owned that status. By 2005 it was no longer even profitable. The recession didn't help. In 2010 Ford gave up on Volvo altogether, selling it at a substantial loss to Chinese carmaker Geely. "We lost our way," Volvo North America CEO Tony Nicolosi told *Autoweek* in 2013.[3] "We gotta go back to our roots. Society is coming back to what we represent as a brand:

environment, family, safety. We've just been poor at communicating it." Under Geely's ownership and substantial investment—with a renewed focus on safety and reliability—Volvo finally began growing again in 2015. But I fear it may have lost its purpose brand status forever.

Purpose brand makes very clear which features and functions are relevant to the job and which potential improvements will ultimately prove irrelevant. A purpose brand is not solely valuable to the customer in making his choices. Purpose brands create enormous opportunities for differentiation, premium pricing, and growth. A clear purpose brand guides the company's product designers, marketers, and advertisers as they develop and market improved products. As I'll discuss in the next two chapters, having a Job to Be Done as a North Star helps guide an organization to design the right product and experiences to achieve that job—and not "overshoot" in a way that consumers won't value.

Achieving a purpose brand is the cherry on the top of the jobs cake. Purpose brand, when done well, provides the ultimate competitive advantage. *Look no further. Don't even bother shopping for anything else. Just hire me and your job will be done.*

CHAPTER TAKEAWAYS

- After you've fully understood a customer's job, the next step is to develop a solution that perfectly solves it. And because a job has a richness and complexity to it, your solution must, too. The specific details of the job, and the corresponding details of your solution, are critically important to ensure a successful innovation.

- You can capture the relevant details of the job in a job spec, which includes the functional, emotional, and social dimensions that define the desired progress; the tradeoffs the customer is willing to make; the full set of competing solutions that must be beaten; and the obstacles and anxieties that must be overcome. The job spec becomes the blueprint that translates all the richness and complexity of the job into an actionable guide for innovation.

- Complete solutions to jobs must include not only your core product or service, but also carefully designed experiences of purchase and use that overcome any obstacles a customer might face in hiring your solution and firing another. This means that ultimately all successful solutions to jobs can be thought of as services, even for product companies.

- If you can successfully nail the job, over time you can transform your company's brand into a purpose brand, one that customers automatically associate with the successful resolution of their most important jobs. A purpose brand provides a clear guide to the outside world as to what your company represents and a clear guide to your employees that can guide their decisions and behavior.

QUESTIONS FOR LEADERS

- What are the most critical details that must be included in the job spec for your target job? Do you understand the obstacles that get in customers' way? Do your current solutions address all these details?

- What are the experiences of purchase and use that your customers currently have? How well do these align with the requirements of their complete job spec? Where are there opportunities to improve them?

NOTES

1. Source: *PowerReviews*, a provider of ratings, reviews, and question-and-answer technology to more than one thousand brands and retailers

2. I recently read an account of a local restaurateur who rued the great reviews he initially got on Yelp because they drove higher-end foodies to his restaurant in search of discovering a hidden gem. His restaurant was, he pointed out, a *decent* local place. But somehow foodies, who he never intended to attract in the first place, ended up disappointed and wrote bad reviews.

3. Rong, Blake Z. "The Future of Volvo." *Autoweek*, December 29, 2013. http://autoweek.com/article/car-news/future-volvo.

SECTION 3

THE JOBS TO BE DONE ORGANIZATION

The real challenge is how do you get this herd of energy—your team—lining up on a future road map, some of which you can't yet see. Jobs Theory helps you do that. It's crazy powerful, if you get that right.

—CHET HUBER, ONSTAR'S FOUNDING CEO

CHAPTER 7

Integrating Around a Job

THE BIG IDEA

Organizations typically structure themselves around function or business unit or geography—but successful growth companies optimize around the job. Competitive advantage is conferred through an organization's unique processes: the ways it integrates across functions to perform the customer's job.

For much of 2015 I was battling an ailment that stumped my doctors. I'd been through rounds of testing and hypothesis, but they just couldn't figure out what was wrong with me. So I was sent to the Mayo Clinic for a week of specialist appointments to see if they could get to the root of my problem. The best way to describe it is the nerves in my body got inflamed and got mad at me. At the time, I was in near constant pain and my trip to the Mayo Clinic was a bit of a blur. But in hindsight, I realized that the clinic had perfectly integrated the experiences and helped me overcome obstacles to getting my job done, something I had never noticed before in years of visits to other medical facilities.

Unlike the situation at a traditional hospital, the Mayo Clinic puts somebody in charge of the process. So, for example, when someone like me comes for a diagnostic visit, that person thinks about all the medical specialties that are involved, which are most likely to have the best insight, and in what order I'd be likely to need to see them. That process person will set up the appointments—sometimes in real time—for me to see all the right specialists while I'm there in that one visit. Every specialist is required to keep openings in the day to accommodate real-time needs. The person in charge of my visit took all the burden of figuring out who I needed to see, what data they'd need for that appointment, which groups of specialists needed to talk to me together, and so on. She made it her problem to move me seamlessly through the day. So as I was barely getting through the day in my pain, someone else was making sure that if I had to see a certain specialist at 2:00 in the afternoon, my MRI was completed by 11:30 at the latest. Whatever anxieties I might have had navigating that visit—*"Will I see everyone today? Is it going to take two months for a follow-up? Does my insurance cover this extra appointment?"* and so on—were eliminated before they could even form into a thought in my mind.

On the surface, the Mayo Clinic is organized around the specialties of the doctors, like many other health organizations. But really, the main organizing principle is a *process* to get the right things in the right sequence to get the job done.

When you think of the word "process" you might instantly conjure images of a manufacturing assembly line or a bureaucratic standard. But processes touch everything about the way an organization transforms its resources into value: the patterns of interaction, coordination, communication, and decision making through which they accomplish these transformations are *processes*. Product development, procurement, market research, budgeting, employee development and compensation, and resource allocation are all accomplished through processes. Helping customers have a delightful experience using your product is made up of processes. *What information do we need to have in order to decide what to do next? Who is responsible for each step? What do we prioritize over other things?*

Resources, generally speaking, are fungible. They can be bought and sold. Products can, often, be easily copied. But it is through integrating *processes* to get the job done that companies can create the ideal experiences and confer competitive advantage.

By contrast to my experience at the Mayo Clinic, in a traditional hospital, there would be a personal-care physician to coordinate my care. He would coordinate it, with the best of intentions, so that every patient has a different experience. But that's different than having a deliberate *process*. The hospital wants to help everybody so badly, but that help comes in an ad hoc way: everyone goes through a different sequence of who they see when. So, for example, whenever there appears to be something going on at the confluence of two different pathways in my body, it can take months, and a series of separate appointments, before I can get the two right specialists in the room together. It is clear, from my personal experience, that it is much easier and faster for good doctors to get answers when they work at the Mayo than when they work in a traditional hospital setting.

Processes are invisible from a customer's standpoint—but the results of those processes are not. Processes can profoundly affect whether a customer chooses your product or service in the long run. And they may be a company's best bet to ensure that the customer's job, and not efficiency or productivity, remains the focal point for innovation in the long run. Absence of a process, as is the case with most traditional hospitals, is actually still a process. Things are getting done, however chaotically. But that's not a good sign. W. Edwards Deming, father of the quality movement, may have put it best: "If you can't describe what you are doing as a process, then you don't know what you are doing."

THE SECRET SAUCE

For years, Toyota freely opened its doors to competitors. Twice a month, the Japanese auto manufacturer allowed rival auto executives and engineers into its manufacturing complex to observe how Toyota makes cars. Not only were the executives allowed to see every aspect of the famous Toyota Production System, the tours also included a robust question and answer session. *Nothing was off-limits.*

To an outsider, Toyota's openness might seem shocking. After all, the American rivals were clearly trying to learn Toyota's secrets in order to emulate or even improve upon them. Why would Toyota so willingly give competitors a hand?

Toyota wasn't really worried that it would give away its "secret sauce." Toyota's competitive advantage rested firmly in its proprietary, complex, and often unspoken processes. In hindsight, Ernie Schaefer, a longtime GM manager who toured the Toyota plant, told NPR's *This American Life* that he realized that there were no special secrets to *see* on the manufacturing floors. "You know, they never prohibited us from walking through the plant, understanding, even asking questions of some of their key people," Schaefer said. "I've often puzzled over that, why they did that. And I think they recognized we were asking the wrong questions. We didn't understand this bigger picture."

It's no surprise, really. Processes are often hard to see—they're a combination of both formal, defined, and documented steps and expectations and informal, habitual routines or ways of working that have evolved over time. But they matter profoundly. As MIT's Edgar Schein has explored and discussed, processes are a critical part of the unspoken culture of an organization.[1] They enforce "this is what matters most to us."

Processes are intangible; they belong to the company. They emerge from hundreds and hundreds of small decisions about how to solve a problem. They're critical to strategy, but they also can't easily be copied. Pixar Animation Studios, too, has openly shared its creative process with the world. Pixar's longtime president Ed Catmull has literally written the book on how the digital film company fosters collective creativity[2]—there are fixed processes about how a movie idea is generated, critiqued, improved, and perfected. Yet Pixar's competitors have yet to equal Pixar's successes.

Like Toyota, Southern New Hampshire University has been open with would-be competitors, regularly offering tours and visits to other educational institutions. As President Paul LeBlanc sees it, competition is always possible from well-financed organizations with more powerful brand recognition. But those assets alone aren't enough to give them a leg up. SNHU has taken years to craft and integrate the right experiences and processes for its students and they would be exceedingly difficult for a would-be competitor to copy. SNHU did not invent all its tactics for recruiting and serving its online students. It borrowed from some of the best practices of the for-profit educational sector. But what it's done with laser focus is to ensure that all its processes—hundreds and hundreds of individual "this is how we do it" processes—focus specifically on how to best respond to the job students are hiring it for. "We think we have advantages by 'owning' these processes internally," LeBlanc says, "and some of that is tied to our culture and passion for students."

Unlike resources, which are easily measured, processes can't be seen on a balance sheet. If a company has strong processes in place, managers have flexibility about which employees they put on which assignments—because the process will work regardless of who performs it. Take, for example, consulting firm McKinsey & Company, which is hired to help companies around the world. McKinsey's processes are so pervasive that consultants from very different backgrounds and training can be "plugged" into the processes by which they habitually do their work—with confidence that they will deliver the needed results. They can also churn the resources—the consultants—every few years without fear of diminution of quality because their processes are so robust.

Putting Jobs to Be Done at the center of your process changes everything about what an organization optimizes for. Before refocusing around jobs, for example, SNHU would have measured success in responding to prospective student inquiries in terms of weeks. *"How many packages got mailed out?"* SNHU would then wait for interested students to follow up with a call. If they did, SNHU would ask them to chase down their historic transcripts to get to the next phase of consideration. And so on. The impetus for the process was left in the hands of the prospective student. SNHU simply responded. By traditional measures, the "cost" of acquiring that prospective student was relatively low and it was easy to staff an office that simply mailed out packages of information.

By contrast, SNHU now tracks response time in minutes. The goal is to call back in under ten minutes. While on the phone with a trained admissions representative, the prospect will be asked to give permission to chase down existing transcripts— and SNHU will pay the usual ten-dollar fee incurred to do that. Success is now measured in whether the university can come back to the prospect with transfer-credit determination and all other necessary information in a matter of days. But it's far, far more successful because it's focused around the prospective student's Job to Be Done. Talking to a live human being, within minutes or hours, is a completely different experience from arriving home after a long, hard day at work to find a big white envelope nestled among the junk. The real payoff for SNHU is in successful acquisitions. If prospective students believe SNHU fulfills their Job to Be Done, they'll stop shopping around—and gladly pay a premium price for the solution that best solves their job.

There's another important lesson in the story of SNHU's success: it systematically *removes* the complexity and frustrations from the prospective student—such as navigating the financial-aid process and tracking down transcripts—and resolves them through the structured processes of SNHU. This is what processes aligned with customer jobs do: they shift complexity and nuisances *from* the customer *to* the vendor, leaving positive customer experiences and valuable progress in their place.

Without the clear job spec of SNHU's students' Jobs to Be Done, the university would never create such a high-intensity process, but nor would it be as productive. Nor would any standard operating data suggest it should. SNHU's old system might have generated, for example, the number of information packages sent out compared with the number of new student applications. But nothing about that ratio would tell the university *why* that number is good or bad. By contrast, the right job spec leads to the right processes that will generate the right data to know "How are we doing?" Jobs Theory focuses you on helping your customers do their jobs, rather than narrow internally measured efficiencies.

ORGANIZING AROUND THE JOB

It's the rare exception that a senior executive visiting my office isn't in the midst of some kind of corporate reorganization—or complaining that it's time for another one. What's striking to me is that these reorgs are not rare, they are remarkably common and in many companies have almost become a routine part of the business cycle: every three to four years a new wave of changes affecting job responsibilities, reporting lines, spheres of authority, P&L ownership, and decision rights—just to name a few dimensions of change—rips through many major companies promising a better future.

More often than not, though, these painful restructurings fail to deliver desired results. A 2010 Bain & Company study reported that fewer than one-third of major reorgs reviewed delivered *any* material improvement and many actually destroyed value.[3] Why would managers ever put themselves through the hardships and hassles and endless meetings and conference calls—not to mention opportunity costs—endemic to reorgs? There's clearly a widespread dissatisfaction with current performance.

Jobs Theory suggests that all this effort is focused on the wrong things. You don't have to sit through many board meetings or strategic planning sessions or acquisition-integration meetings to determine that the focus of most organizational restructurings are the boxes and lines on the org chart, signifying defined roles and reporting lines. Of course it's necessary to have an organizational structure that helps navigate the complexity of running a business. You need experts in finance and marketing and customer service and so on, and you need a way to organize reporting lines and P&L responsibility. But there's something critical missing in these discussions.

Through a jobs lens, what matters more than who reports to whom is how different parts of the organization interact to systematically deliver the offering that perfectly performs customers' Jobs to Be Done. When managers are focused on the customer's Job to Be Done, they not only have a very clear compass heading for their innovation efforts but they also have a vital organizing principle for their internal structure.

This is not a subtle distinction. We have managers in charge of every major function or set of activities. We have executives in charge of product lines. But in most cases, nobody is in charge of understanding—and ensuring that the company is delivering on—the job of a customer. It's only through predictable, repeatable processes that organizations can fully integrate around a customer's Job to Be Done.

Intensive care medicine offers a perfect example. In 1952 surgical pioneer Dwight Harken (who also happens to be the grandfather of coauthor Taddy Hall) noted that, while patients were routinely surviving increasingly complex surgical procedures, alarming numbers were dying in post-op recovery because patients were simply transferred from the surgical theater back to the general wards. There simply was no set of processes to ensure that fragile patients in critical care would receive the array of interventions required for survival. In short, the critical-care job had no owner within any one of the hospital's established medical functions.[4]

The radical question Harken asked himself was, "How is it that everyone's doing what they're supposed to be doing, all of the hospital's existing processes are functioning as designed—yet patients are dying?" Something wasn't right. In posing the question, Harken created the space in his mind to continue to seek and find the answer. His ensuing insight enabled him to pioneer the concept of intensive care medicine as we know it, leading to the now ubiquitous intensive care unit that we've come to take for granted. This was only possible by the realization that the hospital's preexisting processes were failing to deliver desired patient experiences—in this case, successful surgical recovery and survival.

My colleague at Harvard Business School, Ethan Bernstein, spent two years away from HBS working with Elizabeth Warren to set up the Consumer Financial Protection Bureau (CFPB) in the aftermath of the financial crisis. Armed with Jobs Theory, he made a conscious choice to try to avoid the org chart trap. The promise of the CFPB was to bring the tools and authorities into one place so that the fragmentation of responsibilities that some believed allowed the financial crisis to go uncorrected would not continue into the future.

The focus of the CFPB was around consumers' Job to Be Done—in essence, to "know before they owe"—but Bernstein and the CFPB Implementation Team took it a step further, consciously designing the organization structure of the bureau to *support* that job. "It just seemed natural," Bernstein says now. "Instead of seeing divisions, we saw Jobs to Be Done."

With a clear Job to Be Done for consumers who had been badly burned in the financial crisis at its center, it became clear that some of the typical DC functional silos didn't make sense for the CFPB. Research, markets, and regulations were organized in a single division. Supervision, enforcement, and fair lending in another. In a typical regulatory structure, these groups would have all had slightly different—and occasionally conflicting—missions. Enforcement, for example, is all about punishing the bad guys and repairing the past. Supervision, by contrast, might focus on pre-empting future problems by forming close relationships with those being supervised. Traditionally, that represented not only very different approaches, but also very different processes. But put into the same division, people with very different backgrounds, career tracks, and world views were aligned around a similar job: prevention of future consumer financial issues and restitution of past ones. "The organizational structure, and the collaboration processes we put in place helped to create co-identification with professional identities and the CFPB's Job to Be Done," Bernstein says.

For example, the CFPB's policy committee, comprising senior levels of staff from across the entire bureau, met once a week for two hours. That conversation, Bernstein says, was entirely focused on one of the organization's Jobs to Be Done and what tools were going to be used over time to understand and address it. The meeting was run, perhaps not surprisingly considering Elizabeth Warren's background as a Harvard professor, more or less like a Socratic law school class. The conversation focused on the organization's Job to Be Done, but everyone was invited to bring their expertise and opinions on how best to solve it with the issues at hand that week. "If you don't have that focus," Bernstein recalls, "then you start falling into individual opinions and politics. The organization thrived in the early days because we brought in all kinds of people—consumer advocates, Wall Street veterans, other government agency staff. But everyone in that room had scars. If you *didn't* focus around a Job to Be Done, then you focused on the scars. You'd just sit there and argue with each other and get nothing done. Solving a job was our unifying cause. Our reason for being. It was easy to rally around that. And we got action, rather than typical DC paralysis, as a result." Jobs Theory provided a diverse team with a language of integration, enabling diverse functional specialties to communicate and interact to fulfill the ultimate purpose of the CFPB.

WHAT GETS MEASURED GETS DONE

Jobs Theory changes not only what you optimize your processes to do, but also how you measure their success. It shifts the critical performance criteria from internal financial-performance metrics to *externally* relevant customer-benefit metrics. SNHU tracks how many minutes it takes to respond to an inquiry, for example, because it realizes that time is critical to the process of its online prospects. Amazon focuses on when orders are *delivered* not when they are *shipped*. For each new product, Intuit develops a unique set of performance metrics based on the specific *customer benefit* that the specific Intuit solution delivers.

Keeping what matters in focus is challenging for any organization, especially with the forces at play as a company grows. "Now that we're a much larger company, it's been a challenge to keep the various parts of the company focused on the *customer benefit,*" says Intuit founder Scott Cook. "It's so tempting for parts of the organization to start looking at other things. In our kind of business, you get all this data about 'conversions' and 'retention,' and so on. We got seduced by that." It is, to be sure, easier to focus on efficiency rather than effectiveness. Most businesses are very, very good at that. Creating the right metrics is *hard*. But so important.

For example, Cook recounts, as Intuit was rolling out a new version of QuickBooks for small businesses, the sales organization suggested that trial users be forced to register before they could access and test the product. "Why not force them to call us? That way we can sell them more stuff," Cook says. "Buy our payroll service!" On the surface, testing suggested it could be the source of immediate new revenue for Intuit. So the company set up an internal process to field the registration calls and try to upsell them more services. "But it turns out, we made it hard for customers to register. Now they had to call us. Sometimes the line was busy. They had to talk to a salesperson when really they just wanted to register. People got focused on revenue instead of delivering the customer benefit." But that line revenue number, Cook says, can be deceiving. Yes, maybe Intuit converted some of those callers to other products or services. New revenue. But that number doesn't take into account how much of that revenue Intuit might have gotten anyway if it had focused better on solving customers' jobs, rather than the jobs of salespeople to generate new sources of revenue.

If Intuit wanted to accurately measure how well the company was responding to customers' Jobs to Be Done, it needed to find new ways to think about it. *How much time did we save this customer? Did we allow them* to not *spend time doing something they didn't want to do? Did we improve their cash flow? Are our processes supporting the things customers are hiring us to do?*

But measuring the success in achieving these goals is not easy, Cook admits. "This is hard stuff in our business. The metrics don't fall out of our systems. There is no way to continuously and automatically measure the labor hours avoided by accountants. We have to interpolate survey and server data," Cook says. "Because without it we just don't know how we're doing on the job the customer wants done."

Having the right measurements in place helps institutionalize a process. It's how your employees know they're doing the right thing, making the right choices. As the old saying goes, "What gets measured, gets done." From its inception, Amazon has laser-focused on three things that solve customers' jobs—vast selection, low prices, and fast delivery—and designed processes to deliver them. Those processes include measuring and monitoring how it's achieving those three ultimate goals on a minute-by-minute basis. The end goal is getting the customers' jobs done—everything works backward from there. "We always start with the customers and look at all the metrics that matter for the customer," explains Amazon's senior vice president for international retail Diego Piacentini.

Think about the signal sent by this simple line on every Amazon product page, for example: *"If you order within the next 2 hours and 32 minutes, you'll receive your product Tuesday."* But hundreds of processes have been designed to ensure that happens. The customer's click of the "checkout" button triggers a series of processes that extend all the way to the fulfillment center or to the vendor. Amazon then tracks and measures if it meets its promise. Did it arrive tomorrow, as promised?

Process acts as a sort of the subconscious of an organization—it subtly pushes companies toward or away from a Jobs to Be Done–aligned strategy by governing thousands of decentralized events, decisions, and interactions each day. "We're much more focused on processes than organization," says Piacentini. "It's one of the reasons we can move fast. We have the same technology, the same platform, the same guiding principles across all of our companies." New innovations at Amazon famously start with a mock "press release" that is presented to the team that will consider and work on that innovation. The press release contains the guiding principles for that innovation—all experiences and processes are derived from the clarity of what job customers will hire this product or service to do, as outlined in the press release at the innovation kickoff meeting. In that room are not just marketing people, but engineers, analysts, and so on—everyone whose work will play a role in fulfilling that Job to Be Done. "It all starts with that press release," Piacentini says. "No matter who owns the pieces of the product, you're part of that process."

The textbook definition tells us that process optimization relates to efficiency. But what Jobs Theory—and Amazon's example—says is, "Yes, but . . ." The "but" is that optimization should also incorporate a factor for job alignment—otherwise you're focusing on getting better and better at the wrong things.

There is a second very important lesson in the Amazon story: there is a degree of ambidextrousness that enables processes to be *both* highly efficient *and* flexible. Jobs are not flexible—they have existed for years and years, even centuries. But how we *solve* for jobs varies over time. The important thing is to be attached to the job, but not the way we solve it *today*. Processes *must* flex over time when a better understanding of customer jobs calls for a revised orientation. Otherwise you'll risk changing the concept of the job to fit the process, rather than the other way around.

Interestingly, this principle of a modular internal-process structure in which some pieces persist and others change is fundamental to what computer coders know as subroutines. The idea is that repeated functions—say basic arithmetic and trigonometry, for example—can be coded as subroutines and then essentially copied and pasted wherever that operation is called for in a different process. In programming, this is a very big deal. The right use of subroutines will decrease the cost of developing and maintaining a program, while simultaneously improving its quality and reliability. Solutions to common challenges are not invented ad hoc by programmer X or Y sitting at a desk in the basement. They're universal, logical, and easily inserted in the right places.

Amazon has imported what are essentially subroutines into its operating processes, too, and their power and efficiency are very apparent. This is a huge advance over the traditional practice of "sharing best practices" across regions. Instead, the use of subroutines poses the question of "Are we likely to need to repeat this process (or subroutine) in other activities?" This creates a very dynamic view of an organization as a collection of processes wherein each process is a string of subroutines—some custom and some modular imports—that align perfectly with a customer's Job to Be Done.

Aligning with jobs is considering what "process optimization" means. In so doing, you avoid the trap of allowing today's critical processes to become tomorrow's inhibitors to growth.

HIRING ONSTAR FOR PEACE OF MIND

I have a friend who has never been particularly bothered about cutting it too close for a plane departure. I don't think he's ever arrived at the airport more than a few minutes before the gate is scheduled to close. But it doesn't bother him enough to change his pattern; somehow it always works out. Once when I was dropping him off at the airport, I was doing the worrying for both of us. Somehow in the hurried moment of getting him to the right door, we managed to lock the car doors with the motor still running. And we saw, suddenly, that his wallet had fallen out of his pocket and was in plain sight on the passenger seat. He couldn't get on the plane without the identification in that wallet. I panicked and started looking around for rocks to possibly smash in the window to get to his wallet. And then it hit me: we have a subscription to General Motors OnStar. Within a few moments, we were able to borrow a phone to call OnStar and our car was unlocked from outer space, my friend's wallet was retrieved, and I was waving him goodbye— with my car still fully intact. I don't think I'd ever actually used my OnStar service before that moment, but in that moment I deeply appreciated its value.

I can't imagine the complexity of designing a system that can identify my particular car, wherever it may be, from a phone call— and then remotely unlock my door in a matter of seconds. It wasn't by accident that OnStar, the service that provides subscription-based communications, in-vehicle security, hands-free calling, navigation, and remote diagnostics systems throughout the United States and Canada, could solve my problem in that exact moment of struggle. It's a marvelous product.

There are a million reasons it shouldn't have succeeded, but it did. At one point OnStar generated annually, by my estimate, $2.5 billion in revenue and about $500 million in net profit for General Motors with *negative net assets*. During his fourteen-year tenure as CEO of OnStar at GM, Chet Huber and I spoke frequently about the challenges he faced and the obstacles he overcame. He and I were classmates at Harvard Business School back in the 1970s and I'd followed his career with interest. At the time, I thought the usual corporate barriers to a truly breakthrough division would be impossible to surmount at culture-bound General Motors, but to his credit, Huber found a way. He didn't use the language at the time, but in hindsight, Huber says, OnStar succeeded because it focused relentlessly on the Job to Be Done. Everything fell into place from there.

At first OnStar was designed as a kind of Chinese menu of many random cool things that GM and its initial partners in the venture could put into the service to demonstrate synergies among the joint-venture companies. The company would create features and benefits that made for good press coverage at the annual auto shows—things such as "intensity discharge lighting" that would allow you to see seven miles down the road or night-vision systems that had been used in the military. The goal was to get buzz and make the brochure look good, Huber says, but it didn't really matter if a lot of customers actually bought them. OnStar initially was only intended to be the "coolest brochure ware ever."

That made it fun to build. The OnStar team assembled all the features and benefits it could make work and bundled them into the initial offering to customers. It was all singing, all dancing: if you are just looking for a good Italian restaurant for a break on a long road trip, you could push the OnStar button in your car and be given recommendations for the best options. Or you could get routed on back roads through a traffic jam. Somewhere buried on that list of benefits was the concept of a truly integrated communications system in your vehicle. If you have an accident, for example, it will immediately alert emergency services. Or if you lock yourself out of your car, you can call OnStar and it will remotely unlock it for you.

The OnStar team conceived of this as a high-end service, suitable for luxury cars. Akin to adding a fabulous stereo system or leather seats. Except things didn't go exactly as initially planned. GM's CEO at the time, Rick Wagoner, decided that the OnStar division would not get any internal credit for helping sell cars. That was not the goal. OnStar had to create a sustainable business model of its own and a product that customers could actually be willing to pay for. If it had any hope of creating the profitable business Wagoner had challenged it to build, it needed to understand what exactly it was actually selling—and what customers were buying.

At first, the OnStar team couldn't really make sense of how and why customers were hiring OnStar. They'd fool around with it: "We're on a long road trip and we're having a debate we can't settle. Can you name the seven dwarfs?" or the creepier "What are you wearing?" It was a toy. And a toy that lost its charm soon after it was out of the box. People started canceling, noting that they didn't really need the concierge service after all. It was nice, but not necessary.

And there was one other surprise. Not only did some of the luxury car owners start canceling the service, but there was also an unexpected customer base as well. It turned out Chevy drivers, historically the budget-conscious segments of GM's market, were just as likely to purchase OnStar as Cadillac buyers. Those two segments overlapping on the OnStar made no sense to the team. To get to the bottom of it, Huber required every member of his then three-hundred-person OnStar team to spend an hour listening in on real customer calls with the call center team.

They may have grumbled about the extra work at first, but what the team members heard in those hours of monitoring would change everything. The team members who weren't normally part of the call center were shocked at the pressure those employees were under—and the size of the problems they were trying to solve. The OnStar system would trigger when people had just been in an accident. "Our OnStar team would find themselves right in the middle of horrific crashes. In some cases the cars hadn't even stopped moving yet, people were screaming. Or they'd get hit again in a ricocheted series of collisions."

Understanding those moments—the circumstances of struggle—became critical to uncovering the real Job to Be Done for customers. "When you realize that directions are much less about 'find me a good Chinese restaurant' and much more about 'I'm in an unfamiliar location and it's dark. Can you route me through safe streets?' it changes how you approach not only the design, but the way we interact with our customers in those situations," Huber says.

OnStar was being hired to provide peace of mind when you're driving. A whole series of ideas flowed from that crystallization of the Job to Be Done. Imagine that it's 2:00 a.m. and you're on a long drive. Think about what would happen if your "check engine" light comes on in your car. Can I keep driving? Will the engine blow up? Help me decide what to do right now. "That service is much more valuable to you than a diagnostic that tells you how your gas mileage is performing," Huber says. So not only does the technology need to be able to communicate what's going on in your engine to the OnStar service, the call center representatives also need to know how you're feeling when that light comes on and what you need to hear. Understanding the Job to Be Done also demystified the surprise of Chevy buyers subscribing to OnStar at the same rates as Cadillac buyers: peace of mind is an essential, not a luxury upgrade.

By necessity, the OnStar team had to create a panoply of processes to deliver experiences consistent with that specific job. And it took rapid iterations to improve things—something that was not common in the glacially moving auto industry. For example, the processes GM had invented to support the dealers, who were the front line of sales, were terrible. It started with how hard it was to explain OnStar to customers in the showroom. How did this work? Was it hooked to satellites or did it require a cell phone? Did somebody always know where the driver was? Can somebody eavesdrop on the car without the driver knowing it? There were hundreds of questions that could easily derail a sale—and the salesmen were not likely to be motivated. One sale would gain the dealership a 20 percent cut of ten dollars in monthly service fees, nothing more than pocket change to car dealers who could make more adding heated seats to a sale, and be done with their responsibility, rather than selling hundreds of OnStar subscriptions.

"You don't have the luxury of thinking that you've done it perfectly the first time," Huber says. "There's so much at stake and you're learning as you go. This is the source of your competitive advantage. Your processes have to get better and better, based on what you're learning. And all of it has to align with the job your customers are hiring you to do."

Perhaps most significant of all in differentiating the OnStar product was the process that Huber and his team navigated to continually upgrade and improve the OnStar technology being installed in cars. In the auto industry, it can typically take three to five years to develop and bring a new car to market and then it's likely to stay in the market as is for up to ten years. The long window of development and sale is intended to ensure that new cars are thoroughly vetted and tested before they reach the public and then they're efficiently manufactured and produced for a long time. Technology typically rapidly iterates and improves so that each successive generation is of higher quality and cheaper to produce. Huber knew that vetting upgrades and improvements to OnStar through GM's established validation test cycles would be the kiss of death. Nobody wants to buy last year's hot technology this year.

While Huber knew next to nothing about wireless technology when he took over what would become the OnStar division of GM, he did know that any successful wireless product-development cycle would have to move much, much faster than the usual automotive life cycle. "My suggestion very early on was that unless we could suspend those rules, then we shouldn't even bother with the business, because we'd end up selling eight-track tapes when everyone else was selling CDs," says Huber.

That was an incredibly complex process—and it had to work in not just one car model that offered OnStar. It had to work in *all* of them. That meant testing and considering every possible combination of how the system could be used, under what conditions, and in conjunction with whatever else could possibly be happening with the car. *What if all the windows in the car were down? What if it was pouring rain? What if the driver had the CD player on? Would it work if the airbag had been deployed?* "We had to validate it working with every different mechanism in the vehicles," Huber recalls. "And every car was different." The first round of validation involved testing OnStar in hundreds of scenarios. But as the OnStar team continually improved the product itself, there were literally thousands of validation tests that needed to be run. The existing GM validation system couldn't possibly handle that outside of its regular cycles.

So the OnStar team created its own processes to make that happen out of sequence—a first for the auto giant. Working with the existing validation teams, OnStar developed midcycle processes and tests and used its own staff's expertise to ensure that the upgraded product met GM's overall quality standards. Making this process work was a really, really big deal.

That allowed OnStar to continually upgrade the versions of OnStar it offered in its cars. Even when competitors opted to buy the OnStar technology for their automobiles, their own processes couldn't compete with the internal GM team's ability to validate and test new versions in GM's cars. So competitors' cars might be offering version three of OnStar while GM cars were on to the far superior fifth-generation version.

What OnStar built in its first years was not a product that competitors couldn't copy, but a set of experiences and processes that perfectly aligned with customers' Jobs to Be Done. And that, it turned out, was exceedingly hard. In 2000 Ford announced a joint venture with Qualcomm to create Wingcast, a competitor to OnStar, with a promise to be in the market by 2003. Ford didn't focus on the Job to Be Done as OnStar did, but rather suggested that Wingcast would be the next great thing in mobile connectivity. That never happened. Ford scrapped the project two years later. It simply couldn't match the processes that GM had already developed to solve customers' jobs through OnStar.

Ford's core mistake—of focusing on the *product spec* rather than the *job spec*—gets repeated all the time. In fact, the misstep is so common in the high-tech world, that Anshu Sharma of Storm Ventures has earned justifiable recognition for calling attention to the problem, which he has dubbed "stack fallacy." Stack fallacy highlights the tendency of engineers to overweight the value of their own technology and underweight the downstream applications of that technology to solve customer problems and enable desired progress. "Stack fallacy is the mistaken belief that it is trivial to build the layers above yours," Sharma says. It's the reason that companies fail so often when they try to move up the stack. "They don't have first-hand empathy for what customers of the product one level above theirs in the stack actually want. They're disconnected from the context in which their product will actually be used."

Stack fallacy applies outside of the technology sphere, too. For instance, it might be easy for you to have a vegetable garden. You know what herbs and vegetables you like—and all you have to do is to learn how to grow them and use them in your own cooking. On the other hand, your understanding of growing and using herbs does not prepare you to open and run a restaurant. In fact, eight out of ten restaurants fail within five years. Knowledge of production, Sharma says, is not the same thing as knowing what customers are looking for.

In short, stack fallacy and Jobs Theory shine light on the same hazard: to mistake technical know-how—which Ford and Qualcomm had in spades—for the customer's Job to Be Done, about which they understood very little. The high-stakes consequence is to dismiss the specific customer application as trivial when it is, in fact, essential. By contrast, Huber and his team maintained clear focus on the Job to Be Done. They invented, reinvented, and reinforced an entire set of processes to ensure that they were delivering peace of mind to customers. By 2009 OnStar, by itself, had become a key reason that people bought certain GM cars.

Processes are powerful. By their very nature, processes are set so that employees perform tasks in a consistent way, time after time. They are meant not to change. When processes are organized around the customer's Job to Be Done—optimized to facilitate the progress and deliver the experiences that customers seek—processes are the source of competitive advantage.

Over the past six years, FranklinCovey has doubled revenue and increased profit tenfold by shifting focus from selling its own products—training modules—to optimizing customer business outcomes. Historically, FranklinCovey operated like a typical training company. It created content that potential customers, such as sales people, would find useful and designed courses that enabled client training managers to perform their job of offering sales training to their employees. But it discovered that training budgets are highly vulnerable in tough economic times. This is where jobs played a critical role. Over time FranklinCovey transformed itself from, say, focusing on supplying sales training tools to focusing on enabling sales transformation. "We took responsibility for helping our customers to achieve their business goals," says CEO Bob Whitman. Having identified critical Jobs to Be Done for its customers, FranklinCovey is now focusing on perfecting how to integrate the right processes within the company to make sure they deliver on that job for every customer, every time.

"Jobs gives you a very clear innovation trajectory," Whitman says. "I can see how we need to improve for the next ten years. It's less product oriented now than process oriented." For example, Marriott was willing to devote nearly ten full-time employees on its staff to implementing the FranklinCovey "4 Disciplines of Execution" program. But not every customer will have the resources to do that. So FranklinCovey is figuring out how to make it cheaper, faster, and easier to roll out. "Two-thirds of our R&D budget is spent on process innovation," Whitman says. The goal is to create offerings that shift complexity out of the client's process, making the experience of using FranklinCovey's products easier. "It's no good if they thought they signed up for an exercise class and realized once they got there, they had to commit to climb Mount Everest!" Whitman says.

The converse is equally true: when processes are *not* aligned with a compelling customer job, optimizing the process means getting better and better at doing the wrong thing. There's a reason that the fast-food company didn't implement the changes that Moesta and his colleagues recommended to boost milk shake sales. It may have been a great idea, but the organization's "immune system" rejected it out of hand. Local managers deemed the required changes in their routine processes and resource allocations too difficult to implement and the idea died a quiet death. Many smart companies unwittingly undermine their own great ideas with hidebound processes.

This is a good thing when the processes are perfectly aligned with the Job to Be Done. But as OnStar demonstrated, introducing new processes to an established organization is very, very hard. Often the solutions you must deliver seem impractical from a financial perspective or cumbersome from a cultural perspective. As I'll discuss in the next chapter, even the most perfectly constructed experiences and processes are vulnerable to powerful forces within a company. The gravitational pull of existing process is very, very strong. But forewarned is forearmed. In the next chapter we will focus on how to ensure that your processes align with the Job to Be Done and deliver results for both your customers and your shareholders.

CHAPTER TAKEAWAYS

- As we've said in the last chapter, the key to successful innovation is to create and deliver the set of experiences corresponding to your customer's job spec. To do this consistently, a company needs to develop and integrate the right set of *processes* that deliver these experiences. Doing so can yield a powerful source of competitive advantage that is very difficult for others to copy.

- Despite the value of developing a set of processes integrated around the customer's job, it does not come naturally to most companies. Processes abound in all companies, of course, but in most cases they are aimed at improving efficiency or achieving a narrow outcome within a specific function. Delivering a complete set of experiences to nail the job usually requires that new processes be deliberately defined, and new mechanisms put in place to coordinate functions that are usually siloed.

- A powerful lever to drive job-centric process development and integration is to measure and manage to new metrics aligned with nailing the customer's job. Managers should ask what elements of the experience are the most critical to the customer, and define metrics that track performance against them.

- Most organizations do not have one person who is the "steward" ensuring the company consistently delivers against the customer's job. Traditional organizational structures and siloes do have value and are likely to endure, and large-scale reorgs are not usually practical. Therefore, the best way to move toward a more jobs-centric organization is to carefully set up and integrate the right processes, measure the right things, and over time embed jobs centricity in the culture.
- How you solve for a customer's job will inevitably change over time; you need to build in flexibility to your processes, to allow them to continuously adapt and improve the experiences you deliver.

QUESTIONS FOR LEADERS

- How does your organization ensure that the customer's job guides all critical decisions related to product development, marketing, and customer service?
- Do the different functions that are part of your customer's experience (for example, your product, service, marketing, sales, after-sale service) all support nailing your customer's job in a coordinated, integrated way, or are they in conflict?
- What new processes could you define to ensure more integrated delivery of the experiences required by your customers' jobs?
- What elements of the end-to-end experience are most critical to perfectly solving your customer's job? What metrics could you define to track performance against these elements?

NOTES

1. Regarded as one of the most influential management books of all time, *Organizational Culture and Leadership* by Edgar Schein transforms the abstract concept of culture into a tool that can be used to better shape the dynamics of organization and change. Schein, Edgar H. *Organizational Culture and Leadership*. San Francisco: Jossey-Bass, 1985.

2. Catmull, Ed. "How Pixar Fosters Collective Creativity." *Harvard Business Review*, September 2008. https://hbr.org/2008/09/how-pixar-fosters-collective-creativity. Catmull, Ed, and Amy Wallace. *Creativity, Inc.: Overcoming the Unseen Forces That Stand in the Way of True Inspiration*. New York: Random House, 2014.

3. A 2010 Bain & Company study of fifty-seven major reorganizations found that fewer than one-third produced any meaningful improvement in performance. Some actually destroyed value.

4. In his 2009 book *The Checklist Manifesto*, Harvard Medical School professor Atul Gawande chronicled dramatic improvement in patient safety simply by virtue of creating and following a process—checklists—in patient care. Gawande, Atul. *The Checklist Manifesto: How to Get Things Right*. New York: Metropolitan Books, 2009.

CHAPTER 8

Keeping Your Eye on the Job

THE BIG IDEA

The day a product becomes real and hits the market, everything changes for managers. There's so much pressure to grow that it's possible to lose sight of why customers hired you in the first place. Even great companies can veer off course in nailing the job for their customers—and focus on nailing a job for themselves. In our research and experience, that happens because companies fall into believing three fallacies about the data they generate about their products: The Fallacy of Active Versus Passive Data, The Fallacy of Surface Growth, and The Fallacy of Conforming Data.

People don't want to buy a quarter-inch drill. They want a quarter-inch hole.

It's a profound insight—first popularized by legendary Harvard marketing professor Ted Levitt decades ago.[1] Customers don't want products, they want solutions to their problems. Peter Drucker, too, warned us that the customer rarely buys what the company thinks it sells him. There is, as these two sages pointed out, often a profound disconnect between the company and the customer.

These are the two most important marketing insights of the last century—and I don't know many marketers who would disagree.

But the marketers' actions tell us something different.

We believe that most successful organizations are founded, de facto, on this perspective—essentially they identified a Job to Be Done. But after companies have successfully launched, the wisdom of Levitt and Drucker seems to fade away.[2] Something shifts. Even in some of the best companies, the Job to Be Done that brought them success in the first place can somehow get lost in the shuffle of running and growing the business. They define themselves in terms of products, not jobs. And that makes a very big difference.

Most consumers in North America and Western Europe know the brand V8. It is made from the juices of eight vegetables—hence the brand name, V8. It was introduced in 1933. Campbell's Soup Company bought the V8 brand in 1948, and it still resides there.

In the juice-and-drink aisle of our local supermarket, V8 is juxtaposed right up against its nemesis, tomato juice. Going down the aisle you see other competitors—like juices of grapes, oranges, grapefruit, carrots, and pomegranates. About half of the shelf space is occupied by bottled waters from exotic places like Poland Spring, Maine, the glaciers in Iceland, springs in the Fiji Islands, and the public water taps in Ayer, Massachusetts. Gatorade G, which used to be called just plain Gatorade, is there too, holding its own against Powerade. In the next aisle are other sweet drinks, including Coca-Cola and Pepsi, and Red Bull. If this variety is not enough, you can walk down the street to Starbucks, where you can get a latte, cappuccino, Frappuccino, or macchiato.

Ladies and gentlemen, competition in the market for juices and drinks is *tough*. And differentiation is even harder. By definition, the market for drinks cannot grow much faster than the population—meaning that one brand can only grow by scraping it from the hide of direct competitors.

To differentiate their product in this crowded category, years ago the product managers of the V8 brand developed the slogan "I should've had a V8"—connoting that V8 is a refreshing alternative to its neighbors on the supermarket shelf. Occasionally, and inspired by this slogan, I have tried to differentiate myself by buying a can of V8—whose mix of tomato, beet, carrot, celery, lettuce, watercress, parsley, and spinach juices truly differentiate the product and the people who drink it. It has not been a bad slogan. After all, V8 is eighty-three years old and it still goes to work every day.

About ten years ago, out of the blue, a gentleman knocked on my office door and introduced himself as one of four members of the group that manages the V8 brand at Campbell's Soup. He said that the group had read an early article that we had written about the concept of the Job to Be Done. He explained that indeed the group had framed its task as differentiating Campbell's product against all the other drinks and juices. But the concept inspired them instead to inquire whether there was a job that arises in people's lives on occasion for which they might hire V8. They found one. Through the eyes of one of his customers, it went something like this:

> When I was old enough and moved away from home, I promised my mother that I would always eat my vegetables. But I am a busy man. As I peel this stupid carrot and boil that limp spinach and wonder why in the world Popeye likes it so much, I now rue the day that I promised my mother that I would do this. It takes so much time to prepare this food that tastes awful.
>
> Then I realized that if I drink a V8 every day, I can call my mother while driving my car and drinking my vegetables, and report that I am eating my vegetables, just as I promised.

When seen through a Jobs lens, V8 need not compete against Diet Coke and cappuccino. It can compete against vegetables! And just as the milk shake wins the game of commuting hands down against bananas and bagels, V8 wins hands down against peeling carrots, boiling spinach, and flossing celery strings out of your teeth.

The management team quickly changed the advertising to juxtapose V8 against peeling and boiling carrots in the life of a busy man. My visitor later reported that in less than a year, V8 sales had quadrupled. Competing against apple juice is tough. Competing against celery is like going downhill on ball bearings. And V8 became a perfect purpose brand.

What subsequently happened? It's a heartbreaker. I don't know all the internal workings, but I understand that members of the team moved on. I suspect the Job to Be Done was lost in the shuffle. In any case, something clearly changed.

So today when you roll your cart down the juice-and-drinks aisle, this is what you'll see, if the retailer stocks the full V8 line: V8, Spicy Hot V8, Lemon V8, Picante V8, Roasted Chicken V8, Low-sodium V8, Organic V8, V8 *Splash!* (made from fruits, vegetables, *and high fructose corn syrup*), V8 V-Fusion + Tea; and several other variants of variants. Almost overnight, the organization seemed to reorient the business by product line, competing again against other juice and drink products with a bloated product line that creates confusion, not clarity. Without clarity in the purpose brand, customers must ask themselves, "What job does a V8 do?"[3]

If Yogi Berra were still with us, he might read Ted Levitt's adage that customers want a quarter-inch hole, not a quarter-inch drill; then read this history of V8; and observe, "This is déjà-vu all over again."

Why?

THE THREE FALLACIES OF INNOVATION DATA

Even great companies veer off course in nailing the job for their customers and focus instead on nailing the job for themselves. In our research and experience, that's because companies fall into believing one of three fallacies:

- The Fallacy of Active Versus Passive Data
- The Fallacy of Surface Growth
- The Fallacy of Conforming Data

Let me explain:

1. The Fallacy of Active Versus Passive Data

When a company—or product—is first launched, it is usually steeped in the context of the job it discovers. And having uncovered a job with no good solution, it's often competing with no one. Entrepreneurial energy, focus, and resources can be devoted to understanding and solving customers' jobs. But after the company or product has been launched into the world, its energy, focus, and resources turn in a different direction.

Consider the world of discount retailers. This industry is organized not around a job, but around products and price points. As a consequence, over the last twenty years, the field has been very, very crowded. We've seen Walmart, Target, Kmart, Ann & Hope, Costco, Marshall's, Woolworth, Zayre, Bradlees, and Caldor, to name just a few, fight tooth and nail for dominance. There was almost no expectation that all these retailers would survive in the long run. It was a bare-knuckle brawl, a survival-of-the-fittest test based on who could sell the most stuff. There was no way, in advance, to predict who would win. When I first wrote *The Innovator's Dilemma* two decades ago, Kmart was the big deal. Now it's a shadow of its former self. Walmart, Costco, and Target have prevailed, it turns out. And even as these three have won the battle of attrition, no customer on the planet has a Job to Be Done called *"I really need to spend a couple of hours going to the store today."* Consequently, companies organized around a brick-and-mortar business model rather than a customer job are unlikely to thrive over the longer term. Increasingly, they will find themselves playing defense rather than profitably expanding.

By contrast, consider recent success stories like OpenTable, Salesforce.com, Airbnb, or enduring successes such as craigslist or IKEA. Each of these businesses is very clearly organized around a distinct Job to Be Done and each has enjoyed sustained success with minimal competition. It's a totally different game.

This is not a new phenomenon. As Ted Levitt pointed out in the pages of *Harvard Business Review* decades ago, the railroad industry did not decline because the need for passenger and freight transportation declined. That need actually grew, but cars, trucks, airplanes, and even telephones stepped in to handle that job nicely. The railroads were in trouble, Levitt wrote back in 1960, "because they assumed themselves to be in the railroad business rather than in the transportation business."[4] In other words, the railroads fell into the trap of letting the product define the market they were in, rather than the job customers were hiring them to do. They organized and tracked and measured themselves as if they were in the business of selling drills, not quarter-inch holes.

By contrast, many successful start-ups do start out selling quarter-inch holes. The original kernel of the idea for Netflix was uncovered the way many start-ups gain traction: an entrepreneur found himself in a circumstance with no clear solution and declared, "I'm going to fix this!" In a sense, he began both as the CEO and a target customer— there was no separation between the innovator and his customer's job. Much of the information needed to make decisions about solving for a job is found in the context of the struggle. We call that "passive data" because it has no voice or clear structure or champion or agenda. Passive data, by itself, doesn't tell us what is going on in the world because the Job to Be Done doesn't change much. Passive data is just unfiltered context. It's always present, but it isn't loud.

In discovering an unfilled or poorly done job, managers are surrounded by nonconsumption and workarounds. They are immersed in the passive data of context. Familiar marketplace markers such as product sales, quality standards, and competitive benchmarks are all missing. Instead, signposts of innovation opportunity take the form of individual customers' frustrations and undesirable tradeoffs and experiences. Making meaning out of the jumble of real-life experiences is not about tabulating data but about assembling the narrative that reveals the Job to Be Done. Innovators have to immerse themselves in the messy context of real life to figure out what potentially successful new products might offer to customers. In the early stage, managers are puzzle solvers, not number crunchers. Passive data does not broadcast itself loudly. You have to seek it out, put clues together, relentlessly ask *why?* But it's critically important because it is the way to identify innovation opportunities.

Here's how the trouble starts: managers by their very nature respond to information—and negative information, in particular, causes them to respond quickly.

We can predict, however, that, as soon as a Job to Be Done becomes a commercial product, the context-rich view of the job begins to recede as the active data of operations replaces and displaces the passive data of innovation. Once products are launched, a faucet is opened and data is created, data that didn't exist until sales had been made and customers created. Managers feel an understandable sense of reassurance when they shift their attention from the hazy contours of *a story of struggle* to the crisp precision of a spreadsheet. And this switch happens organically and with little fanfare:

1. Product sales generate *data about products*: how many, how profitable, and which ones, etc.
2. Customers' purchases generate *data about customers* themselves: business or consumer, large or small, wealthy or not-so-much, direct or via sales channel, local or far-flung, etc.
3. Investments in people, facilities, and technology generate *data on their productivity, returns, and value.*
4. Competitors emerge, leading investors and managers to create *benchmarks that make data.*

This data, as it turns out, is very loud. It shouts at you to focus on it and prioritize it and improve it. It's easy to track and measure and is usually seen as a proxy for how well the manager is doing his job. This is a subtle but transformational shift in perspective, and it feels good to migrate from the unstructured messiness of passive data to the reassuringly concrete active data.

But what feels like progress can prove to be poison if it leads managers to mistake the model of reality that active data offers for the real world.[5] Data is *always* an abstraction of reality based on underlying assumptions as to how to categorize the unstructured phenomena of the real world. Too often, managers conveniently set this knowledge aside: data is man-made.

As data about operations broadcasts itself loudly and clearly, it's all too easy—especially as the filtering layers of an organization increase—for managers to start managing the numbers instead of the job.[6] A great illustration of this is the way public schools in America teach so their students will pass the requisite tests because the government depends on schools hitting certain measured standards. Or in medicine, consider how doctors often treat symptoms, rather than getting to the cause of the problem. High blood pressure, for example, is a symptom of several different diseases. But most drugs for people who struggle with high blood pressure focus on getting those numbers down, rather than curing what's causing them in the first place.

Companies do this, too. They manage the numbers. Think about the correlation between earnings per share and the price of your shares in the market. If a company goes into the market and repurchases some of its own shares, it can improve the earnings per share and the stock price often goes up. But it's done absolutely nothing to make the company more innovative or more efficient. The number went up. Period.

2. The Fallacy of Surface Growth

When a company makes big investments in developing relationships with customers, natural incentives arise to find ways to sell more products to existing customers. The marginal cost of selling more products to existing customers is very small—and the profit is oh so alluring. We call this "surface growth." Companies see products all around them made by other companies and decide to copy or acquire them. But in doing so, companies often end up trying to create many products for many customers—and lose focus on the job that brought them success in the first place.[7] Worse, trying to do many jobs for many customers can confuse customers so they hire the wrong products for the wrong jobs and end up firing them in frustration instead. This makes companies vulnerable to disrupters who focus on a single job—and do it well.

The same incentives and logic apply to investments in production capabilities, intellectual property, and talent. Once these costs are sunk, the pressure to "sweat the assets" is ever present and, especially with "what have you done for me lately" shareholders, relentless.

The *New York Times* offers a good illustration. There are two customers who matter to the *Times*: readers and advertisers. In the case of readers, there are lots of jobs that arise in their world—and the *Times* tries to do more and more jobs for the same set of customers. For example:

- Help readers unwind at the end of the day.
- Provide readers with up-to-date news.
- Help readers become informed.
- Help readers fill their time productively.

But with each additional job that the *Times* solves, it finds itself up against a competitor who focuses only on that job—and does it very well. The *Economist* is a great way to feel informed with one weekly briefing, rather than having to spend time on getting informed every day. Nothing's simpler than turning on the television to relax in the evening—with many more choices about what you want to watch. The *Metro* newspaper that readers get for free on the subway helps readers fill their time productively on their commute, and so on. Suddenly the *Times* has a handful of competitors—in addition to other mainstream media—who are solving its customers' jobs better than the *Times* can. It's no surprise that so many newspapers have found themselves struggling to survive in recent years. They weren't focused around a job. By contrast, Deseret News Publishing Company, which I'll discuss in depth in the next chapter, has staged a stunning turnaround by reorienting its traditional newspaper along a very distinct Job to Be Done.

3. The Fallacy of Conforming Data

The Fallacy of Conforming Data is the third fallacy that causes companies to lose their focus on the customers' Job to Be Done. Data has an annoying way of conforming itself to support whatever point of view we want it to support. In fact, Nate Silver, a well-known statistician and founder of the *New York Times* political blog FiveThirtyEight (it was acquired by ESPN in 2013), noted, "The most calamitous failures of prediction usually have a lot in common. We focus on those signals that tell a story about the world as we would like it to be, not how it really is."[8] We don't realize this, we don't mean for it to happen, but it is an unfortunate frailty of the human brain.

Psychologists have explained that when we hold conflicting ideas or beliefs in our minds, this "dissonance" produces reactions of stress and anxiety that we naturally seek to minimize and avoid. Uncomfortable truths are just that—uncomfortable. As data comes in, it's not that we *lose* objectivity—we never had it to begin with. I can't help but think of every parent-teacher conference I ever attended—my wife and I would always leave the room with totally different perspectives on what we just heard. I heard, I'm sure, the things that confirmed my expectations. My wife, I suspect, heard something closer to what the teacher actually said. We make the data and the messages conform to what we believe.

So often, companies are blindsided by a competitor's innovation or what turns out to be a missed opportunity. *"Why didn't we see that coming??"* The truth is, you had no chance of seeing it because you weren't looking for it. In the words of Sherlock Holmes, "There is nothing more deceptive than the obvious fact."

Does this sound familiar? Your sales, marketing, and R&D teams are all in the same room with the business-unit head, discussing where to focus innovation resources. The sales team is sure it knows what customers want because it's constantly talking to its customers about their most pressing needs. The marketing team has reams of ideas for leveraging the existing brand, perhaps by offering new versions, new flavors, new colors, or special offers. The R&D team is excited about new features and benefits it's working on, driven by cool new technologies or applications. And the head of the business is relentlessly focused on getting things into the market that have a shot at helping the P&L by the end of the year. Needless to say, each team comes armed with carefully constructed supporting data that offers a model of reality through the lens of its functional responsibilities, performance metrics, and financial incentives. All the teams are working with a kind of confirmation bias—seeing only the information that tends to support their point of view. None of these perspectives is wrong, but the point is that none is truly objective. And more important, not one of the models reflects the customers' job.

We pick and choose the data that suits us. "Decisions don't get made. They happen," observes neuromarketing expert, Gerald Zaltman, a longtime colleague at Harvard Business School who has spent years studying how managers represent their ideas and apply their ideas and knowledge. Among the common mistakes he's identified? "The tendency to treat facts as insights and leap directly from data to action," Zaltman recently wrote in the *Journal of Advertising Research*. "It is common when research is used to prove points rather than as fuel for imaginative insight."

In fact, Zaltman says, we often kid ourselves about just how objective our decisions are. "It might look like a leader has made a big decision—A versus B—when in fact, in all the layers that led up to that decision, the data has been increasingly skewed toward A. A leader may think they've made a leap of faith based on clear data, but in reality, it's already been kind of pre-ordained." Innovations get skewed to do the jobs that *executives* want them to do—which is to confirm that the customers want to buy the products that the managers want to sell them.

THE SOURCE OF DATA CREATES THE PROBLEM

There's an even more fundamental problem with data. Many people view numerical data as more trustworthy than qualitative data. But where does "objective" data come from? The data used in many research projects comes from companies' financial statements, for example. Is this objective? H. Thomas Johnson and Robert S. Kaplan showed quite convincingly that the numbers representing revenues, costs, and profits in financial statements are the result of processes of estimation, negotiation, debate, and politics in allocating overhead costs that can produce grossly inaccurate reflections of true cost and profit.[9]

The healthiest mindset for innovation is that nearly *all* data—whether presented in the form of a large quantitative data set on one extreme, or an ethnographic description of behavior on the other—is built upon human bias and judgment. Numerical and verbal data alike are abstractions from a much more complex reality, out of which a researcher attempts to pull the most salient variables or patterns for examination. Whereas the subjectivity of data from field-based, ethnographic research is glaringly apparent, the subjective bias of numerical data hides behind its superficial precision. Tom Monahan, who built practice-insight and technology company CEB into a billion-dollar publicly traded company, joked with me that with his earnings one of his dreams is to endow the Museum of False Precision. It promises to boast a well-stocked collection.

Data is not the phenomena. The primary function of data is to represent the phenomena—to create a simulation of reality. But there is a misconception about data that is so prevalent it's tacitly embedded in many organizations—the idea that only quantitative data is *objective.* There's a pervasive belief that there is some set of ideal data that can, together, yield the perfect insights about customers. It's just a matter of figuring what the right data is. In short, we can know "truth" if we just gather the right data in *quantitative* form, the kind of information that can be fed into a spreadsheet or regression analysis. *How many? What? Where? Who? When?* By contrast, qualitative data—observations and insights that don't fit neatly into a spreadsheet to be sliced and diced—is not as reliable as quantitative, because there's no single "truth" at the core. Quantitative data, the thinking goes, is somehow better.

But that's not correct. Deity does not create data and then bestow it upon mankind. All data is man-made. Somebody, at some point, decided what data to collect, how to organize it, how to present it, and how to infer meaning from it—and it embeds all kinds of false rigor into the process. Data has the same agenda as the person who created it, wittingly or unwittingly. For all the time that senior leaders spend *analyzing* data, they should be making equal investments to determine *what* data should be created in the first place. What dimensions of the phenomena should we collect data on and what dimensions of the phenomena should we ignore?[10]

In the spring of 2014 *Science* magazine published the findings of an academic study of the popular Google Flu Trends[11]—Google's flu-tracking service, which is supposed to predict flu trends ahead of the traditional Centers for Disease Control and Prevention reports. Google Flu Trends (GFT) was based on an algorithm that matched fifty million search terms against 1,152 data points. In essence, Google hoped to predict flu outbreaks by cross-referencing search terms (symptoms, medical providers, remedies) with relevant objective data. The authors, academics from Northeastern University, Harvard University, and the University of Houston, concluded that Google Flu Trends had wildly overestimated the number of flu cases in the United States for more than two years. The article, "The Parable of Google Flu: Traps in Big Data Analysis," concluded that the errors were, at least in part, due to the decisions made by GFT engineers about what to include in their models—mistakes the academics dubbed "algorithmic dynamics" and "big data hubris."

Google had admirable goals: maybe early warning on flu trends could prevent the spread of disease and save lives earlier than conventional methods. But as Google engineers found, you have to make choices about what to analyze. Unfortunately, the exact link between specific search terms and Google's algorithm was far too complicated and subject to myriad human dynamics (maybe a hypochondriac searched the same terms month after month or perhaps Google engineers shifted the way data was collected from time to time, and so on . . .) to provide a reliable predictive tool.

Because terms from searches on Google are created on computers and can be stored and analyzed in many new ways, they have the appearance of a valid data set, but are not. Just because the phenomena—in this case, searches—can be computed and analyzed does not mean that they deserve the status of data. Is it directionally helpful? Yes. Is is objective reality? No.

PASSIVE DATA NEEDS ACTIVE MANAGEMENT

Are companies doomed to veer off a jobs course when their normal operating systems kick in—watching the competitive advantage they worked so hard to gain slip away? Not if senior leaders protect themselves and their organizations from falling prey to the Three Fallacies of Innovation Data. But it will absolutely, positively happen if the customer job is not given a voice and a champion. Passive data needs active management. We turn to this challenge in the next chapter, "The Jobs-Focused Organization."

CHAPTER TAKEAWAYS

- The origin story of most companies typically involves an entrepreneur identifying an important job that does not have an existing satisfactory solution, and developing a creative way to solve it.

- As a company grows up, however, it's very common for it to lose focus on the job that sparked its existence in the first place. Despite the best intentions and a century of marketing wisdom, companies start to act as if their business is defined by the products and services they sell ("quarter-inch drills") instead of the jobs that they solve ("quarter-inch holes").

- While there are many drivers of this drift away from the true north of the customer's job, foremost among them is the tendency of managers to fall prey to the Three Fallacies of Innovation Data:
  - *The Fallacy of Active Data Versus Passive Data:* Instead of staying cognizant of and focused on the type of data that characterizes the rich complexity of the job (passive data), growing companies start to generate operations-related data (active data), which can seduce managers with its apparent objectivity and rigor but which tends to organize itself

around products and customer characteristics, rather than Jobs to Be Done.

- *The Fallacy of Surface Growth:* As companies make big investments in customer relationships, they focus their energies on driving growth through selling additional products to those customers or solving a broader set of their jobs, what we call surface growth—as opposed to staying focused on solving the core job better.
- *The Fallacy of Conforming Data:* Managers focus on generating data that conforms to their preexisting business models.

- Awareness of these fallacies is the first step toward preventing them from taking over innovation in a company, but doing so on an ongoing basis requires constant vigilance and intervention.

Questions for Leaders

- How connected are your innovation efforts to the core jobs your company was started to solve?
- How would your people characterize the fundamental business you are in? Would they describe it in terms of solving an important job in their customers' lives, or in terms of the products and services you offer?
- What data drives your innovation and investment decisions? How closely connected is this data to your customers' jobs?
- Are you falling prey to the Fallacy of Surface Growth, that is, are you overly focused on driving growth through selling new products to existing customers without an understanding of the progress customers are trying to make in their lives?
- What data is gathered and presented to make important innovation and investment decisions? What mechanisms do you have in place to ensure that this data reveals what you need to see, rather than what is comforting to believe?
- How are you ensuring that your customers' Job to Be Done has a voice in your decision making and resource allocation activities?

NOTES

1. Levitt is commonly credited with this insight. But in his book *The Marketing Imagination*, he attributed it to Leo McGinneva. Levitt was undoubtedly, however, the one who popularized the term. Levitt, Theodore. *The Marketing Imagination*. New York: Free Press, 1986.

2. The entire time I was an MBA student at Harvard Business School, I never heard the quarter-inch hole or selling customers the wrong things mentioned. Not when I was a student, not even after that when I was working at Boston Consulting Group, and not even during my doctoral studies. I only inadvertently heard someone refer to the whole analogy much later in my career—and rued not learning it sooner. How could something so profound become so obscure?

3. I had a great exchange of ideas with the gentleman who visited me that day. Even though he freely shared his story with me, I have chosen to protect his identity here. But the publicly available facts about V8 speak for themselves.

4. Levitt, Theodore. "Marketing Myopia." *Harvard Business Review*, July/August 1960.

5. By analogy, look at our health care system. My cardiologist never calls me because the data about my heart doesn't change. I'm happy to say it's healthy. There's no active data to respond to. But that illustrates why we have a system that only treats sickness—it's not a "health" care system; it's a "sick" care system. They're not the same thing. When we get sick, all of a sudden the data about us that the doctors see kicks into high gear and the system organizes around making that data look better. But that's not the same thing as keeping us healthy in the first place. This is the same thing that managers do—they respond to changes in data, but don't pay attention to the passive data that is steeped in the context of the most important thing the manager should be focusing on: the customer's jobs.

6. Many economists assume a rational actor in their models, because people have access to all needed information and thus can act rationally. But in reality, we rely on the information that is created by the situation that we are in—as Nobel Prize winners Herbert A. Simon and James G. March explore in their explanation of "bounded rationality." Bounded rationality is the idea that in decision making, the rationality of individuals is limited by the information they have, the cognitive limitations of their minds, and the finite amount of time they have to make a decision.

7. A good example of this is the power-tool line DeWalt, which had earned its reputation through its stellar radial arm saw. It was the best in the industry—and it helped establish DeWalt as a brand you could trust. But after Black & Decker acquired it in the 1960s, DeWalt spread into new areas. It seemed to me that Black & Decker just went up and down the aisles of the hardware store to see what everybody else was making—drills and clamps, and so on—and thought, *Oh, we can do that, too. It will create new revenue.* DeWalt then found ways to outsource the manufacturing of these new products so they could be produced inexpensively. But trying to steal revenue from your competitors by taking them on with lower-quality imitations is not a growth plan to count on. That's why we call it surface growth. You can copy ideas you already see on the shelves but none of this is based on a clear understanding of jobs—and it's far, far less likely to succeed.

8. Silver, Nate. *The Signal and the Noise: Why So Many Predictions Fail—But Some Don't.* New York: Penguin Press, 2012.

9. Johnson, H. Thomas, and Robert S. Kaplan. *Relevance Lost: The Rise and Fall of Management Accounting.* Boston: Harvard Business School Press, 1987.

10. I know firsthand the limits of what data tells us. Our son Michael graduated from Harvard Business School as a Baker Scholar, the highest academic honor given to MBA students. If you look at the data about him while he was at HBS, it would probably list

the courses he took, the grades he got, and his attendance record. But what it wouldn't record is that he was the "education representative" for his section of the class. It was his responsibility to cultivate a culture of learning and supporting each other within the section. It was, I believe, a truly great section, in part because of what Michael did as its leader. I think it was the most powerful lesson he learned at HBS, how to inspire people by creating the right culture. But there's no data to reflect that. That data is all embedded in the context.

This reminds me of a moving speech by Bobby Kennedy:

"Our Gross National Product, now, is over 800 billion dollars a year. . . . Yet the Gross National Product does not allow for the health of our children, the quality of their education, or the joy of their play. It does not include the beauty of our poetry or the strength of our marriages, the intelligence of our public debate or the integrity of our public officials. It measures neither our wit nor our courage, neither our wisdom nor our learning, neither our compassion nor our devotion to our country. It measures everything, in short, except that which makes life worthwhile. And it can tell us everything about America except why we are proud that we are Americans."

11. Lazer, David, Ryan Kennedy, Gary King, and Alessandro Vespignani "The Parable of Google Flu: Traps in Big Data Analysis." *Science,* March 14, 2014.

CHAPTER 9

The Jobs-Focused Organization

THE BIG IDEA

Many companies have lofty mission statements with a variety of intentions from motivating workers to informing strategies to attracting investors, but almost as many companies struggle to translate these mission statements into everyday behaviors. However, when the job has a voice in an organization, individual work streams have meaning and employees understand why their work matters. A well-articulated job provides a kind of "commander's intent," obviating the need for micromanagement because employees at all levels understand and are motivated by how the work they do fits into a larger process to help customers get their jobs done.

Not long ago, Intuit founder Scott Cook led a brainstorming session devoted to improving one of Intuit's flagship products, TurboTax. For years the team has focused on how to improve the "interview" built into TurboTax that asks customers to answer questions and fill in data to generate an accurate tax return. Every year the team would debate how to improve that interview tool, polishing and perfecting and adding specificity that led to the most accurate possible results.

With the well-intended effort of giving customers what they ask for, Cook recalls, Intuit's development teams would extensively survey customers about what new features they'd like to see in Intuit products. And customers had a lot to say. They'd rattle off an expansive wish list. "They'd ask for 150 features," Cook says. So the team jumped on that feedback. Development teams would spend weeks arguing and debating which of the list of potential new features were most important to provide. Everybody, Cook says, was guided by what he or she thought was right for the customer. But in reality, it offered no guidance at all. "We got into feature chase," Cook says. "Too often we'd go look at what customers were asking for and build it." But absent a clear understanding of the job the customers were hiring that product to do, "there was simply no way to differentiate which features were the right ones. It's like navigating without a compass."

Then Intuit promoted a new leader, Sasan Goodarzi, to general manager for the TurboTax organization. It dawned on him that maybe TurboTax had been missing the point. Customers weren't hiring TurboTax to provide them with a better tax interview tool. "Sasan led the organization to a deeper understanding," Cook says, "of 'what problem did the customer really want solved.'" The organization's energy, for years, had been focused on a good goal, but not the goal customers wanted most. Customers didn't want to have to work through that interview at all. They didn't want to have to input data. They hired TurboTax to get their taxes done. Period.

It was a sea change from optimizing the interview to eliminating the need for it altogether. But an energizing one. That realization, Cook says, led to an immediate burst of creativity in the organization. Once the team was focused on the Job to Be Done, it was clear what TurboTax had to be working to solve: completing customers' taxes without their having to answer any questions or input any data.

How is that possible? Goodarzi and his team are still working on solving the challenge, but they've made progress. For example, if a customer gives TurboTax permission to obtain W-2 information from a payroll company such as ADP, a lot of basic information can be downloaded immediately into the customer's tax return. Achieving a true "no interview" TurboTax might take a decade, Cook says, but even the baby steps they've been able to take toward that goal have made a significant difference in customer experience already. In 2015 Intuit experimented with preloaded data, such as payroll information, in just one "chapter" (there are anywhere from four to forty chapters, depending on the taxpayer's situation) in the TurboTax questionnaire. With just one chapter being prefilled in, Intuit saw a noticeable uptick in the number of customers who actually completed the TurboTax interview, even when customers had to manually correct some of the data that was automatically filled in.

In the case of TurboTax, the team had a flawed essential unit of analysis when it focused on relentlessly improving the interview. But this is exactly what most companies do when they follow the wrong innovation guides. How can a leader consistently rally his team about such a challenging goal—and keep them focused? "I think you're on to the sixty-four-billion-dollar question," Cook says. Staying relentlessly focused on the job enables—and even compels—employees to new and better ways of working. A deep understanding of customers' Jobs to Be Done should trigger a cascade of questions about how the company is organized, what's measured and rewarded, what priorities run throughout the company, and how people work together to solve problems. As Cook suggests, we don't yet have all the answers to these questions, but we do know that leaders interviewed for this book have told us that Jobs Theory turns out to be a powerful tool for focusing and leading the organization as a whole. In Intuit's case, Cook says, the organization is so focused on customers' jobs that it allows itself to operate like a "network of start-ups" in which small teams launch new product pilots with minimal senior-level approval because they are so clearly aligned with jobs. When everyone on the team understands that the goal is "taxes are done," they're all pulling in the same direction.

Having a jobs-focused organization, the CEOs we interviewed for this book tell us, leads to four categories of clear benefit:

- Enable distributed decision making with clarity of purpose—employees throughout the organization are empowered to make good jobs-focused decisions and to be autonomous and innovative.
- Align resources against what matters most—and free resources from what does not.
- Inspire people and unify your culture in service of what they care about most.
- Measure what matters most—customer progress, employee contributions, and incentives.

Focusing on customers' Jobs to Be Done provides not just a one-off improvement idea, but an enduring innovation North Star. It helps bridge the gap between what senior management expects to see happen and what rank-and-file employees instinctively know to do. It's both inspiring and empowering.

Most companies have a mission statement—and if they're lucky, employees will have memorized it well enough to recite it chapter and verse. However, mission statements are usually phrased at such a high level and so generically that employees find it difficult to use them as guides for action, decision making, and innovation. Take, for example, these mission statements from a few Fortune 500 companies.

To help all people live healthy lives. (Becton, Dickinson and Company)

To discover, develop and deliver innovative medicines that help patients prevail over serious diseases. (Bristol-Myers Squibb)

Our vision is to realize the tremendous potential of The Burlington Northern and Santa Fe Railway by providing transportation services that consistently meet our customers' expectations. (BNSF [Burlington Northern and Santa Fe])

At the heart of The Chevron Way is our Vision to be the global energy company most admired for its people, partnership and performance. (Chevron)

We aim to be the most respected financial services firm in the world, serving corporations and individuals in over 100 countries. (J.P. Morgan)

These are just a random sample, but they're representative of typical corporate mission statements. There's nothing wrong with having a mission statement. They're like the themes of our lives that I spoke about earlier in the book—*I want to be a good father. I want to be a good husband. I want to contribute to my community.* But on their own, they aren't enough to provide guidance in daily decision making.

But a clear job spec does. For example, unlike the case in the yellow fats business, Unilever has managed to turn the oldest "health" soap brand in the world, Lifebuoy, into one of the company's fastest growing brands in the past few years by nesting a job under the mission of helping children in emerging markets live to the age of five. You can't innovate to the broad goal of helping children live, but you can innovate around the very specific circumstances of that struggle. Experts tell us that it takes thirty seconds of vigorous washing with soap and hot water to eliminate germs—but in the circumstances that Unilever was innovating into, that was not likely to happen. Most people spend around seven seconds washing their hands—and rarely more than fifteen seconds. Kids are usually in even more of a hurry. In emerging markets, the circumstances were even more daunting. In India, for example, nearly 400,000 children under the age of five die in a year from diarrheal disease—an average of more than one thousand deaths a day. Yet mothers and children in parts of India, and other emerging market countries, don't routinely wash their hands.

So Unilever created a series of products that helps consumers make the progress they were struggling to make—in their particular circumstances. Color-changing soap was created to ensure that children scrubbed for long enough to kill germs. The soap changes color when they've reached ten seconds—all that is required to kill germs with Unilever's special formula—(and makes it more fun for kids to stick with it long enough to matter). The mission of saving children's lives was powerful, but it was only with the specificity of what job consumers were trying to do that Unilever was able to energize its oldest soap brand. The more you understand about the job, the better you will connect to it internally.

AN INTUITIVE PLAYBOOK

A leader has to count on employees up and down the company's ranks to make the right choices in everyday decisions. Those choices will determine a company's real strategy. As we discussed earlier, the way an organization's employees work together toward common goals is the basis of its culture. If they work together with a focus on the Job to Be Done, a culture will emerge that reinforces that job and stays deeply connected to it. If that culture has formed around the job, people will autonomously do what they need to do to be successful.

But those instincts aren't formed overnight. Rather, they are the result of shared learning—of employees working together to solve problems and figuring out what works. As long as the way they have chosen keeps working to solve a problem, the culture will coalesce and become an internal set of rules and guidelines that employees in the company will draw upon in making the choices ahead of them. The advantage of this is that it causes an organization to become self-managing. Managers don't need to enforce the rules. They understand the "commander's intent"—a military term that explains why soldiers up and down the ranks know how to make the right choices absent a specific order. They are clear on the commander's goals and priorities.

Business leaders need to ensure that employees everywhere in the company make the right choices every day without requiring constant supervision. This is nothing new: as far back as ancient Rome, emperors would send an associate off to govern a newly conquered territory thousands of miles away. As the emperors watched the chariot go over the hill—knowing full well they would not see their associate again for years—they needed to know that their understudy's priorities were consistent with their own and that he would use proven, accepted methods to solve problems.

A clearly defined job spec that everyone understands can serve the same purpose—a focal point for employees to make the right decisions without being told specifically what to do each time. Absent a specific directive, employees know how to balance the tradeoffs that necessarily come with any new initiative. What's most important? What can't we compromise on? What's the ultimate goal? What's my role in achieving that ultimate goal? Jobs Theory provides you with the right set of lenses to make everyday choices that connect to the jobs you are solving in customers' lives. Jobs Theory provides a language of integration, whereby marketers, engineers, salespeople, and customer service employees can communicate with each other, rather than talk past one another.

As Mercer's Jacques Goulet sees it, the concept of a Job to Be Done serves this purpose perfectly *"because* of its simplicity. It's a simple expression—one-syllable words. Jobs. To. Be. Done. It's not overly engineered and overly complicated. But it's powerful, it's simple, and it focuses the mind."

It's not easy to get these jobs-based goals right—as we've discussed, jobs are complex and nuanced and require a deep understanding of the progress a consumer is trying to make. But when you do, the impact on an organization's productivity can be dramatic, because the resulting clarity enables a much greater share of the organization's human capital to be deployed with the right balance of autonomy and alignment. Since we know that strategy is formed in the everyday choices employees make about resources, processes, and priorities, clarity about what jobs your customers are hiring you to do provides a kind of intuitive playbook.

A TWO-SIDED COMPASS

Once GM's OnStar team figured out that customers were hiring the service for peace of mind while driving, that clarity shifted the organization's focus from cool new "brochure ware" features to genuinely targeted customer benefits that aligned with the Job to Be Done. It was a focus that played out not just in what and how OnStar designed into its service, but the everyday decisions made by employees in all parts of the organization. In an organization like GM, where OnStar was formed, there are potentially limitless possibilities for how a service like OnStar could develop. But should it? Having clarity of Jobs to Be Done actually made it easier to decide what did and didn't belong in the OnStar suite of benefits and services. *What to pursue, what not to pursue? Which technical priorities were most important? Which didn't add value? How do we talk to our customers? How do we make sure dealers aren't obstacles to the job customers are hiring us to do?* "The real challenge is how do you get this herd of energy—your team—lining up on a future road map, some of which you can't yet see. Jobs Theory helps you do that," says Chet Huber, OnStar's founding CEO. "It's crazy powerful, if you get that right."

Until they zoned in on the Job to Be Done, Huber and his team were picking and choosing among all kinds of cool bells and whistles that OnStar *technically* could offer. Optimizing around the Job to Be Done, Huber says, might have seemed to narrow the team's focus in a way that was limiting—but in reality, it provided helpful clarity. Less time and energy were spent evaluating options. "The focus you get greatly simplifies."

For example, Hurricanes Katrina and Rita hitting the Gulf Coast less than a month apart in 2005 triggered a whole series of new experiences and processes essential to keeping the peace-of-mind promise. When Katrina hit, OnStar was new enough that it hadn't had the experience of intersecting with a natural disaster. When the call center started getting flooded with calls, all kinds of previously unconsidered problems were flagged. A panicked customer would call in the middle of getting on the road and be told that their OnStar plan didn't include getting real-time directions. So initially, OnStar required that customers buy an upgrade to access the plan that gave directions.

By the time Rita was approaching, OnStar realized what was happening, that these weren't individual subscriber issues but regional crisis events. And while you couldn't envision any more powerful call to action to buy a service upgrade than being caught in a hurricane, it just didn't feel right to the people delivering the services—it wasn't consistent with the job they were being hired to do. So the employee in charge of that part of the OnStar business simply made a decision to immediately offer anybody calling from a crisis area all the services that OnStar offered, without requiring any upgrades to her current plan. It was so clearly the right decision, Huber says, "it was about a fifteen-second conversation in my office. I can't imagine many organizations in which that would be possible."

Not least because making the decision—and executing it— are two different things. The way the OnStar system had been designed and built at that point made it technically difficult for an employee to just declare that everyone in the affected zone would automatically receive all the services that OnStar offers. OnStar had to create imperfect workarounds—"we had to cobble it together with duct tape and Velcro to make it work," Huber recalls. For example, OnStar had to create a system that would detect all calls coming from a regional crisis area and divert them to a specialized call center team that would have access to valuable real-time information, such as the best evacuation routes or current weather forecasts. Making that happen was not simple. But the difficulty of the challenge never undermined the clarity of its purpose. It gave his team laser focus. As Huber sees it, the Job to Be Done served as a compass.

As was true for Intuit's Cook, Huber found the power of focusing his team around the Job to Be Done extended beyond knowing what features and benefits made most sense. The clarity of a Job to Be Done actually motivated employees to do their best work because they clearly understood why that mattered. When the arrow on the "two-sided compass" shifts to point more clearly at a deeper understanding of the job, so too must the other side of it, aligning with a better job spec.

"Whenever something came up that we had never thought about, but clearly intersected with this compass heading, people just did it. They just got on it," Huber says. "You didn't get the normal reaction, 'Don't give me one more thing to do.'" Instead, Huber says—like what Cook found at Intuit—the team would often be energized by the focus.

Here's an example of the two-sided compass in action. After discussions with emergency room physicians showed that providing 911 responders with advance information about the severity of a car accident they were responding to had the potential to save lives, Huber's team eagerly rallied around that goal with new processes. It was a very difficult technical problem to solve—what information was needed to determine how serious a car accident has been? It would require a complex algorithm and the ability to determine the relevant information automatically. *The change in velocity. The use of seat belts. The direction of the force. How many cars were involved?* And so on. "I remember the discussion with the engineers," Huber recalls. "I was a little bit nervous—it was clearly the right thing to *try* to do, but it was likely to be really hard and very expensive. But in a relatively short period of time, they came back and said, 'We think we can figure this out.' And it wasn't because I told them to go work nights and weekends to figure it out. It was because they knew what was at stake and that it was perfectly aligned with the job we were being hired to do. This wasn't figuring out how to beam latte coupons to Starbucks into the OnStar unit. This would save lives."

As Huber found, a clear Job to Be Done can provide the foundation for an organization's culture—*we solve problems this way because we know what matters and why.*

Southern New Hampshire University's Paul LeBlanc believes his organization's clarity around a job empowers employees to clear the roadblocks for students when they happen. "We have a culture that empowers people to put that to work," he says. For example, a career-services advisory staff member was supporting a student who reported that she was running out of cash. She happened to be a single mom without a huge support network around her at home. That adviser decided on her own to purchase a $200 gift card from a local grocery store to send to the student. In another case, a tech help desk employee and an adviser working with a student who was a few credits shy of graduation, but was very ill, took it upon themselves to present a case to the dean that the student had completed enough work to finish her degree. When they got approval, they personally flew to present her diploma to her while she was in the hospital. "These things happened with no prompting," LeBlanc says. "But they're clearly consistent with the Job to Be Done. My goal is making sure we continue to create the structures and the culture by which people make those right choices without being asked." At its best, Jobs Theory enables "lean" operations—waste and overhead and time are minimized systematically because once you have alignment around the job, LeBlanc says, wasted time, energy, and resources are minimized.

"We had a saying when I ran American Girl," reports American Girl founder Pleasant Rowland, "'American Girl is story, not stuff.' It was a constant shorthand that we used among ourselves to keep us honest about that. I think within the company, you could walk into any part of it and talk to any person and they would tell you that. We were all zealots, we thought we were going to change the world and hold back adolescence for a couple of years." The jobs focus, Rowland says, was constantly empowering employees up and down the ranks. It motivated them. "Everyone who came and worked for me liked the Job to Be Done—making childhood better for girls and for moms."

MEASURING WHAT MATTERS

"What gets measured, gets done." It's generally used in the positive sense of urging managers to measure for benchmarking efficiency and improvements. But the data we use to measure efficiency is double-edged. Yes, it enables measurement and management, but data also creates a model of the external world. Managers inside a corporation—especially large ones—rarely know their customers directly. They know the customer only through data—the models and spreadsheets that slice, dice, and reconstruct real people into "segments" of similarly attributed phenomena. When companies organize themselves into business units with responsibilities for products of certain characteristics or units with responsibilities for certain customer groups, data is gathered through those filters creating models that rarely map to customer jobs.

"Turns out in the modern world, there's so much you can easily measure: screens, traffic, conversion rates, frequency, screens per use. . . . There were so many things to measure that our people got full of measuring all the stuff that was easy to measure because it rolled off our servers," says Intuit founder Scott Cook. But in spite of the volume of data that Intuit had on every click its customers made, something fundamental was missing. "We weren't measuring what was most important to our customers. Because it's hard to measure. But it matters profoundly. We were not measuring whether we were improving customers' lives."

"Improving customers' lives" didn't translate into a single piece of data that Intuit was already capturing. But it was possible to measure whether Intuit was providing the experiences in purchase and use that its customers were seeking in hiring Intuit software. For example, Intuit knows that accountants who hire Intuit software are trying to save time doing clients' tax returns. That frees them up to take on more clients (and consequently bill more) or simply to have more free time to pursue other activities. Did Intuit software help them achieve that?

Cook, who served on the board of Amazon for years, points to the online retail giant as the model of understanding how to measure what matters most to customers' Jobs to Be Done—while still focusing on improving efficiency. As we discussed earlier, Amazon founder Jeff Bezos has been crystal clear since its inception that there are three things that matter in their retail business: vast selection, low prices, and fast delivery. In Amazon's now famous "customer backward" innovation process, those three measures are monitored on a minute-by-minute basis. Bezos doesn't consider delays to be accidents or poor performance, he considers them "defects" to be eradicated. For example, to stay true to its foundational promise of "lowest prices," Amazon built a shopping robot, an automated search engine that scours the prices of hundreds of benchmark products twice a day. If a lower price was found, the Amazon price was automatically lowered to beat that competitor's price. That's why you sometimes see an unexpected price drop while a product sits in your Amazon shopping cart. If the lower price dips below some appropriate gross-margin threshold, it triggers human review. Everything about that system is designed for efficiency—but its focus is squarely on efficiently delivering on the job customers are hiring Amazon to do. Bezos personally hands out the Amazon "Just Do It" award—an old Nike shoe—every few months to an employee who has strayed from his or her official job responsibilities to do something for the greater good of Amazon. That kind of focus keeps employees clear on what matters most to Amazon's customers.

SNHU has a similar focus. "Our success is defined by our students' success," President Paul LeBlanc says. While SNHU tracks reams of data at a micro level, LeBlanc and his leadership team keep one critical statistic front and center: Would graduates of SNHU do it all over again if they had a chance? In essence—did they hire the right "solution" to get their job done? As of early 2016, 95 percent of those surveyed said yes. As LeBlanc puts it: "We can measure lots of things. But *what* you measure matters."

JOBS CHANGED EVERYTHING . . .

The night of the Boston Marathon bombing on April 15, 2013, Clark Gilbert was riveted by the television and laptop screens in his hotel room as the world tried to piece together what had happened in the chaotic aftermath of the bomb. Gilbert stayed up much of the night, watching the breaking news unfold, trying to make sense of the shocking tragedy. But his intense interest in the coverage was not solely that of a concerned citizen: Gilbert was then-CEO of Deseret News Publishing Company,[1] the organization that publishes Utah's oldest daily newspaper, *Deseret News*. The next morning, as he walked the corridors of his hotel to the elevator and through the lobby, he couldn't help but look critically at the rows of newspapers outside of the hotel rooms and in the lobby. They had missed the emerging story because they'd gone to press before critical details had surfaced. Hour by hour throughout the night, more details had been shared, video of the bombing and scores of photos were posted, early misinformation was corrected, and the names of victims and heroes had begun to emerge. An entire news cycle had played out in the interim.

Glancing at the headlines of those newspapers in the hotel lobby was a stark reminder: the jobs that people hired traditional print newspapers to do were far better filled by other sources. There was no newspaper in his hotel lobby that morning—including his own—that would have been the best solution to hire for getting up to speed on the bombing. The 24/7 television news cycle, live blogging on major media sites, and even Twitter had eclipsed them. If you didn't already know that there had been a bombing in Boston the day before, you must have been living in a cave.

That realization was not, of course, a surprise to Gilbert. The newspaper industry had been fighting a losing battle for decades to be hired for the job of breaking news. And Gilbert had been leading *Deseret News* through a reorganization for several years, focusing on building the organization's digital capabilities to better compete in a just-in-time-news world. But the Boston Marathon bombing coverage brought home to him that focusing on building digital didn't address the core question: What job are our readers hiring us to do?

Newspapers had historically been hired to address four to five distinct jobs. For example, the classified ads were targeted at jobs such as "help me find employment" or "help me to find a low-cost item I can buy this weekend." Opinion columns might be targeted at the job of "find someone who supports my view or who can clarify my view." And prior to the revolution in communication speed brought on by the Internet, print newspapers were where people turned to keep them abreast of breaking news stories, or, in

Gilbert's words, the job of "tell me what is happening right now in my community."

But muddling all these jobs together, and doing none of them well, prevented newspapers from understanding what people really were trying to get done—regardless of whether it was through a printed newspaper or an online publication. This key insight would have allowed them to double down on making their solution even more distinctive for these jobs, and enable them to stop wasting resources trying to address jobs for which they were no longer relevant.

If there were a host of better solutions to perform the job of "tell me what is happening right now in my community," was there still a Job to Be Done that *Deseret News* could fulfill—and could it be compelling?

So Gilbert and his team turned to Jobs Theory to answer the question.

What started as a demographic segmentation actually led to a jobs-based segmentation, Gilbert reports. "We found a segment in the country looking to solve a very common job: I want to be well-informed, feel more confident in my knowledge, and still be true to my beliefs so that I can make a difference in my home and community." The target audience was made up of subgroups: tolerant believers (people of faith and family values, but with less of a denominational focus), devoted denominationalists (people of a decidedly religious background), and strugglers (people who might have had aspirations to be in one of the other two groups, but for whom life had been more challenging). Taken together these three subgroups became known collectively as "like-minded believers." They valued family, were generally faith-oriented, worried about the decline in moral values, were focused on teaching their children, and wanted to give back to their communities.

Remarkably, in *Deseret's* research these like-minded believers made up nearly 56 percent of American news consumers and yet they felt massively underserved. Part of the reason that traditional media was missing them is that they couldn't be identified on traditional demographic or psychographic dimensions. They were not primarily rich or poor, Democrat or Republican, or even urban or rural. What distinguished these news consumers is that they had an entirely different Job to Be Done and no one was providing it in the news media. What the mainstream media so often provided was news about the awful, seedy side of life. These news consumers wanted thoughtful, nonpolemical news and analysis from credible sources. But they also wanted that news and information to be informed by issues that mattered to them, including their families, their perspective on faith, and their desire to understand solutions. Gilbert described the frustrated news habits of these like-minded believers by saying: "They were reading the *New York Times* and watching Sean Hannity and they hated them both. They admired the rigor and depth of the *New York Times* but felt a disconnect, even an ignorance of their core values. They heard some of their values from Sean Hannity, but it felt polemic and angry." Into that breach, the *Deseret News* began to meet the Job to Be Done that had been there all along in the American public, but never identified and served deliberately.

The *Deseret News* is an affiliate of the Church of Jesus Christ of Latter-day Saints (LDS), but had historically run itself more or less as a traditional newspaper, competing with other local and national newspapers to be the primary source of news in its local region. Through a functional, emotional, and social lens, the *Deseret* team identified a significant gap between what traditional media (including the historical *Deseret News*) had been providing and what many consumers wanted. "We realized the job was 'be well-informed with news that reflects my values,'" Gilbert says. "People wanted this type of information so they could be more confident in living [their] beliefs and so they could make a difference in their homes and in their communities." They weren't looking for the "shock and awe" value of news. "We knew that if we could deliver against that emotional dimension of the job, they were going to read more and more from us."

Gilbert used this insight to frame the challenge for his leadership team: find a job for which print media is still relevant and can be distinctive, and focus all your energy on nailing that job. "I used to say to people, 'You're going to have to pretend that everyone already knows the story you are writing about. It's old news. That is the context for consumption of anything we might put out in print.'"

Fortunately for the team at *Deseret News*, this line of thinking quickly led them to identify a very compelling job related to getting deeper insight and analysis on news events that had already happened. To describe this job, they borrowed an acronym from the publishers of the *Dallas Morning News*, PICA: "Perspective, Insight, Context, and Analysis." Readers were looking for all these things after an event had already happened and been reported on. In other words, there was still a job focused on helping readers understand the meaning and relevance of a news event after it became known to the public. But that was only the functional part of the job. The emotional part of the job for the *Deseret News* then layered on top of the functional job and helped readers connect those issues to their deeper interests around their families and their faith. "What the *Washington Post* is to DC politics, we want to be for the American family," Gilbert says.

Gilbert's description highlights perfectly the importance of the *circumstance* in framing this job: "We realized that on the functional side, there was still a role for the newspaper when it was last to the game. It's the 'tomorrow morning' circumstance, the circumstance that happens after a story has already been reported and people know the basic facts. People can only listen to CNN repeat the same thing for so long. What we all need the next day is deeper analysis of what it all means."

Clarity on the jobs *Deseret News* could distinctively solve provided not only a compass for how to shape its solutions and how to compete, but also a filter for what to *not* do. Take the example of covering the legislative session in Congress. Traditional news organizations would say, "We're covering the legislature," and provide broad coverage across all the bills and debates happening in the session. But the jobs-based lens resulted in a different approach: "For our A1 page coverage on the legislative session, there might be thirty bills coming forward. But we would focus on just the five issues that were going to affect your family. Once we had this job related to faith and family defined, it completely shaped the way we searched for, discovered, and covered news. It was about understanding the job of the reader—putting yourself in those shoes."

It also had the benefit of clarifying who were the right employees to carry out that Job to Be Done for readers. "We are not the *Sacramento Bee*," became the rallying cry to make that distinction clear. "What I was trying to say was we are not a traditional newspaper. We're not generic. We'd use that to help emphasize what we would *not* do because it didn't align around our Job to Be Done," Gilbert says. "Everyone knew that the worst insult you could get was that a story or a page looked like the *Sacramento Bee*. That would be the last thing you'd ever want said about your work inside the organization."

Not everyone at the existing organization got it, Gilbert says. And some of those employees had to be restructured or counseled out. But on the other side of those changes has come a culture that's focused on the same goals: "One of the reasons we have seen so much growth is that we have been able to recruit and cultivate talented people who believe deeply in the idea that there is a gap in faith and family news coverage in this country."

"Reorienting the whole organization around that job really changed everything," Gilbert says now. *Deseret News* saw dramatic circulation gains relative to its traditional print competitors. It also saw online traffic soar. And it realized it was also addressing an important social dimension of the job as well, which was to connect with like-minded readers. "Once we put that audience together socially, we found huge connections between our readers. It was electric—we put together social communities on the web connected by their common interest in issues related to faith and family."

But rather than building its social communities around traditional publications, the *Deseret* team began building communities around the emotional benefits of the job itself, launching communities on Facebook around faith and family-oriented themes and letting those channels carry the news content to a much wider audience. The number of followers on social media went from the low millions to over 100 million (through a variety of social channels created through *Deseret*'s FamilyShare Network), a number that would shock people who haven't ever heard of *Deseret*. But that, Gilbert and his colleagues say, is tied to the clear Job to Be Done. "We found huge engagement with people who might never have come to us," Gilbert says. "When we built our social strategy around the Job to Be Done versus the product of the newspaper, it opened up our market to a much broader audience than we ever thought possible."

STAYING IN CONTEXT

Every successful organization achieves initial success, consciously or not, by performing a valuable job for a group of customers. At the outset, there is very little in the way of processes or the type of rules we refer to as "priorities," such as how companies evaluate opportunities, compensate managers, and measure success. A successful start-up is typically organized around the job, which tends to make it look like a small group of people each wearing multiple hats and sharing an understanding for what the entity is delivering that enables the customer to make progress. In short, the organizing unit in a start-up is the customer's job.

Things change over time: growth requires additional layers of management and increased communication. Clear individual responsibilities and defined processes are a simple necessity as an antidote to chaos. The informal, often unconscious way that early-stage entities organically organize around the Job to Be Done—because that's how value is created and revenue is generated—becomes untenable and unmanageable as companies grow. Inexorably, the organizing unit moves to a far more intense focus on customers and products and competitors and investors—but a less and less intense focus on the job. Increased control and efficiency, however, is not without risk. The risk is that managers frame their task as efficiently executing established internal processes rather than effectively resolving customers' Jobs to Be Done. And the further removed managers are from the customer context, the easier it is to slip into a highly edited view of the external world.

Over time, our organization can become less and less aligned with the job customers hire us to perform as we blithely expand and optimize our capabilities based on these internally benchmarked "competencies." But Intuit, SNHU, American Girl, OnStar, *Deseret News*, and so many other of the successful organizations we've studied reveal a very different orientation: a focus on the core customer job as the defining and aligning organizational principle of the enterprise.

Functional oversight and efficiency is a requirement of competitive markets. However, efficiency is only value creating when it is in the performance of a process that is creating customer value by fulfilling a high-priority job. Successful organizations pursue operational efficiency without compromising the customer Job to Be Done.

"You might disagree about spreadsheets or marketing campaigns," observes Hari Nair, group chief of the Strategy Innovation Office at the Malaysian-based conglomerate Sime Darby. Nair has used Jobs Theory in his innovation work for years, including in prior positions at Innosight, Procter & Gamble, and Kimberly-Clark. He says, "But internally nobody should be debating about the Job to Be Done. I have seen it be a unifying force in a corporation. We are inundated and flooded with messages, often conflicting. But it's simplifying to say: 'Let's get back to the Job to Be Done. What are our customers hiring us to do?' We don't argue about that."

CHAPTER TAKEAWAYS

- Understanding the most important jobs your company solves for customers can be translated into a rallying cry that aligns individuals across the organization behind a common purpose and functions as an enduring innovation North Star.
- In contrast to the usually generic nature of most companies' mission statements, a well-crafted statement of the jobs a company exists to solve can be both inspiring **and** practical.
- An organization explicitly focused on a clearly defined job enjoys four key benefits:
  - *Distributed decision making:* Employees throughout the organization are empowered to make good decisions that align with the job, and to be autonomous and innovative.
  - *Resource optimization:* The jobs focus shines a light on which resources are aligned against what matters most and which are not, and enables them to be rebalanced accordingly.
  - *Inspiration:* Solving a customer's job is inherently inspiring to individuals in an organization, as it enables them to see how their work enables real people to make progress in their lives.
  - *Better measurement:* With a focus on the job, people will naturally seek to measure and manage to more customer-centric metrics.
- Finding the right way to articulate the job your company is in business to solve—and driving this deeply into your culture—can be difficult and takes real work, but the benefits are worth it.

- What are the most important jobs—or *the* most important job—your organization exists to solve?
- How broadly understood are these jobs across your organization? Are they reflected in your mission statement or other key company communications?
- Do your leaders consistently communicate the centrality of these jobs?
- How could you embed these jobs in all your leadership communications, your corporate communications, and your culture?

NOTES

1. I have previously served on the editorial advisory board of *Deseret News*.

CHAPTER 10

Final Observations About the Theory of Jobs

THE BIG IDEA

In this final chapter I have three hopes. First, I want to convey my enthusiasm for what the Theory of Jobs can accomplish for innovators, because it answers one of the most important questions that has bedeviled managers for decades: Is innovation inherently a question of luck? Our answer is decidedly "no!" Second, I want to convey the boundaries of the theory—what it can explain, and what it cannot. This is critical. If the theory is applied beyond what the theory was designed to explain, it will lose its clarity and predictability. Third, I want to cultivate your curiosity—by showing you through illustration the depth and breadth of questions we can explore through the lenses of Jobs Theory.

CAN WE REALLY CALL THIS A THEORY?

For many who will read this book, the word "theory" connotes a series of equations or a formula that describes how the independent variables or factors affect the outcome of interest. More often than not, the architecture of the research that produces the theory was *deductive* in character. Research in this genre starts with a core proposition of causality, and then searches for data or phenomena that validates (or invalidates) the core proposition.

Other theories are built through *inductive* research. Scholars doing this work start *without* a proposition of causality. Instead, they simply and carefully examine the phenomena and data about the phenomena. Then step by step they develop a proposition about what causes things to occur, and why.

The Theory of Jobs to Be Done was built inductively. Because failure in innovation has been so common, I could not start with a core proposition of causality in successful innovation that I could test in a deductive way. So for two decades I have carefully and inductively observed what people who sold and bought things were trying to do, and tried to get answers to the question, "Why?"

A key goal in building a theory inductively is to develop one or more "constructs." Constructs are rarely directly observable. Rather, a construct is an abstraction—quite often, a visualization that helps observers see how the phenomena interact with and change each other, over time. Whereas correlations reveal static relationships among the phenomena, a construct is a stepping-stone that helps us to see the dynamics of causality.

In chemistry, for example, Auguste Laurent's (1807–1853) visualizations (constructs) of chemical compounds enabled him to explain how compounds arise and are transformed into other compounds. In economics, Adam Smith's construct (1776) of an "invisible hand" helped explain how free markets work. Figuratively, the invisible hand allocates capital and labor to activities that bring prosperity, and it takes resources away from entities that waste them. It has helped billions of people understand how capitalism, properly structured, helps mankind. In the theory of disruption, the key to defining the essence of disruption was being able to visualize trajectories of how technological progress and market needs interact.

Why this diversion into the role of constructs in theories? *The term "job" is a construct.* It fits exactly the definition of what a construct is, and the role it plays in the Jobs to Be Done Theory. Understanding *jobs* as a construct involved carefully defining the terms that I needed to communicate what I had been seeing. The terms "hire" and "fire," for example, are not simply cute words. Rather, they helped me visualize how the processes of buying and selling actually work.

Some who read this book might criticize it because real stories of real people in real companies are not data of the sort that can be manipulated in a spreadsheet. This concern is wrongly applied to the development of good theory. When you see numerical data, remember that it was created by people: individuals or groups of people who decide which elements of the phenomena they include in published data and which they overlook and destroy. Hence, data reflects bias. A wonderful book, *Relevance Lost* by H. Thomas Johnson and Robert S. Kaplan,[1] shows that there is a complicated story behind every number. These stories are hidden when they are parsed and distilled into numbers. When the stories are told, they are *rich* in data. The insights from the right cases are deep. Numbers that were distilled from stories offer insights that are often shallow but broad.

For these reasons, we feel confident that the "Theory of Jobs" is well named.

WHEN THE THEORY IS "WRONG"

A theory never pops out of a researcher's mind complete and perfect. Rather, it evolves and improves as people use it. Good theories actually *need* anomalies—things that the theory cannot explain—in order to improve. The discovery of anomalies forces researchers to dive back into the phenomenal muck. They need to improve the theory so that it can account for the anomaly, or define a new boundary beyond which the theory ought not be used. Each time we discover and account for an anomaly, we learn something more about how the world works.

One of the silliest habits of many in academia is to orchestrate a finding that "disproves" a theory that a colleague has developed and published. The authors publish their paper in a journal of repute, and then smugly lie back on a beach somewhere because their paper is now "in the literature." This helps no one. *Anomalies do not disprove anything.* Rather, they point to something that the theory cannot yet explain. Scholars who find anomalies need to roll up their shirtsleeves and work to try to improve a theory or replace it with a better one.

I hope that you and the other readers of this book will find things that the Jobs Theory cannot yet explain. If you will communicate these problems to me, it will help me improve our collective understanding. At the time of writing, I am developing ways for these theories to be improved collaboratively online and I welcome your thoughts. My deepest thanks, in advance, for joining the quest to learn more and more about the theory, and helping all of us to understand how to manage innovation more successfully.

THE BOUNDARIES OF THE THEORY

Two decades ago, I used the term "disruptive innovation" to describe the phenomena by which entrant companies can topple powerful incumbent companies. The Theory of Disruption has guided tens of thousands of companies toward prosperity. But because, like most words in the English language, "disruption" has many meanings, the Theory of Disruption has also been misapplied. It's been used to describe many phenomena and situations where it actually does not apply. I've puzzled about whether I could have used a better term or descriptor, but have yet to find a better alternative.

For this reason, I would like to try to put boundaries around the word "jobs" as we are using it. It is easy to slip into using "jobs" to describe our attempts to understand a wide range of human motivations. But not everything that motivates us is a Job to Be Done. Jobs, as we've defined them here, take work to uncover and understand properly, thus dubbing something a job shouldn't roll off the tongue with minimal thought. My definition of a job in this book is intentionally precise. I see two problems that you must avoid as you study and apply Jobs Theory.

First, if you or a colleague describes a Job to Be Done in adjectives and adverbs, it is not a valid job. It might describe an experience that a customer needs to have in order to do the job, but it is not a job, as we have defined it here. For example, "convenience" is not a Job to Be Done. It might be an experience that might cause a customer to choose your product rather than a competitor's product, but it is not a job. A well-defined Job to Be Done is expressed in verbs and nouns—such as, *"I need to 'write' books verbally, obviating the need to type or edit by hand."* In contrast, the sentence *"We should aspire to be more honest"* is a noble goal, but it's not a job.

Second, defining a job at the right level of abstraction is critical to ensuring that the theory is useful. This can be more art than science, but there is a good rule of thumb: *if the architecture of the system or product can only be met by products within the same product class, the concept of the Job to Be Done does not apply.* If only products in the same class can solve the problem, you're not uncovering a job.

A couple of examples: *"I need to have a chocolate milk shake that is in a twelve-ounce disposable container"* is not a job. The possible candidates that I could hire to do this are all in the milk shake product category. I could call this a need or a preference—but it isn't a job. We need to go up another level of abstraction in order to discover the job. *"I need something that will keep me occupied with what's happening on the road while I drive. And also, I'd like this to fill me up so that I'm not hungry during a 10:00 a.m. meeting. I could hire a banana, doughnuts, bagels, Snickers, or a coffee to do this job."* The candidates to do the job are all from different product categories; and our rule of thumb is that this is the right level of abstraction.

Another illustration: *"I need a thin sheet of material that we can wrap around a house just before we apply shingles, siding, or bricks. It needs to have a high coefficient of friction; a low coefficient of thermal conduction; and a high coefficient of toughness—so that it won't rip as we wrap the house. Oh—and it also must be impervious to moisture."* This isn't a job, it's a technical specification. It gives me the choice of buying Tyvek by DuPont, or to be cheap, ignore the spec, and use nothing instead.

I need to go up to a higher level of abstraction in order to discover a job. This is what we might find as we explore for it:

"We're building a new house here in Boston, where the cold, damp air of winter and the hot, humid air of summer both easily penetrate walls. I want my family to feel warm and cozy in my home in the winter—and cool and dry in the summer. I need to insulate the outside walls of this house so I can minimize the costs of heating and air-conditioning."

I could hire wood (paper) pulp and blow it into the space in my walls to do this job. I could also hire rolls of fiberglass insulation and staple it to the studs in the wall. Or I could hire Tyvek by Dupont. And to nail things down even tighter, I could hire Tyvek and rolls of fiberglass together. Or I could plan on compensating with extra sweaters in the winter and throwing open more windows in the summer. Maybe I should buy a couple of dehumidifiers and fans. Or maybe I could just hire Santa Barbara or San Francisco, where Mother Nature has obviated the problem of insulation—and I could move there.

We can see that this is a Job to Be Done and not a technical specification or requirement. We know this because the alternatives of things to hire to get the job done come from very different categories of products and services.

DEPTH AND BREADTH OF THE THEORY'S APPLICABILITY

The Theory of Jobs has evolved a lot over the last two decades. Without intending to do it, but in the course of trying to help many different people with many different problems, I have been stunned by how broadly and deeply the Theory of Jobs can be used. Almost every day I become aware of an interesting new example of Jobs Theory in action. My daughter Katie recently regaled me with details of Drybar, a salon in which you can get only one service: a perfect "blowout" for your hair—along with the attendant experiences that help you prepare for a special night out and make you feel good about yourself while you're there. (I had no idea such things were coveted, but I stand duly corrected.) In just a few years, Drybar has become a visible success in cities around the country.

And at the other end of the spectrum, I recently had the pleasure of discussing Jobs Theory with a four-star Air Force general grappling with challenges of motivating and retaining top personnel in an era of government budget constraints. When he left my office, it was as if he saw his dilemma in an entirely new light—one that provided some hope. "Never in my wildest imagination would I have guessed that a story about milk shakes would change the way I thought about recruiting in the military," he declared as we parted company. It's a challenging problem he faces, but I hope Jobs Theory offers him the perspective to make a difference. These are just a few examples that come quickly to mind from recent days. But I've been thinking about using insights from Jobs Theory for some of the bigger problems in our families and our society for a long time, such as in our personal lives, education, and health care.

Happiness at Home

In 2012 Karen Dillon and I joined with James Allworth, one of my most thought-provoking former students, to write *How Will You Measure Your Life?*[2] In its sixth chapter, we put on the Jobs to

Be Done Theory, like a set of lenses, and looked at what goes on in our personal lives. We see things that have been hiding in plain sight in our personal lives and families for many years. We pose questions such as, *"What is the job that our children hire parents to do for them?"* and *"What is the job(s) that my wife needs to get done, for which she might hire a husband?"* These questions are posed at the right level of abstraction. For example, when something breaks in the house a wife might hire her husband to do the job. She could also hire a tradesman to repair it. She might simply do it herself. Or she might just live with it, never fixing the problem. Another job is that she needs to feel loved. She could hire a husband to get this job done. But all too often the husband doesn't do the job very well. So she could hire friends and family to do the job, or her profession to do it. Or she could live her life without ever getting this job done well. We hope you will read this and think about the jobs you are being hired for in your life—and if you are performing them well. It might be a sobering exercise.

Public Education

In 2010 Michael Horn, one of my brightest former students and now a leading voice in the national discussion of the future of education, and I published *Disrupting Class*[3]—an inquiry into why our public schools struggle to improve. Improving schools is a very complicated problem, of course. As we mentioned earlier in this book, one of the most important insights we conveyed in *Disrupting Class* came when we put on the Theory of Jobs lenses and explored what the job is that students are trying to do. We concluded that school is *not* a job that children are trying to do. School is one of the things that children might *hire* to do the job. But the job is that children need to feel successful—every day. And they need friends—every day. Sure, I could hire school to do these jobs. But I could drop out of school and hire a gang to feel successful and have friends. Or I could drop out of school, get a minimum wage job to earn some money, and buy a car—and cruise around the neighborhood with my friends.

Most schools don't do this job well at all. Instead, most children feel failure when they go to class. They could also hire athletics to do the job. For a few, sports do the job well. But for the less gifted, athletics makes students feel failure, too. So they hire electronic games to feel successful. And yet for many, even such games yield failure. So they hire friends who have feelings of failure, too—and engage in drugs and other things to feel successful.

I was heartened to learn recently that Corning CEO Wendell Weeks and his wife, Kim Frock, have set up an alternative school, the Alternative School for Math & Science, in Corning, New York, with the explicit goal of helping children feel successful at school. That's what the Khan Academy is focusing on, too. It gives me enormous hope to know that great people are working on getting the job of students right. We've learned that these important Jobs to Be Done in our children's lives have been hiding in plain sight.[4]

Health Care

In 2009 I teamed with another of my terrific former students, Jason Hwang (now cofounder and chief medical officer of Icebreaker Health), to write *The Innovator's Prescription*[5]—a book to explore why the cost of our health care system increases at an unsustainable rate, even as accessibility declines. Again, a key for unlocking this dilemma has been the Jobs to Be Done Theory. For example, the job of most people is that they want to be so healthy that they don't even have to think about health. Yet, in systems where the providers of care are reimbursed for services they provide, they actually make money when the members of their system get sick—it's effectively "sick care" rather than "health care." When the members are healthy, the providers make little. In other words, the Jobs to Be Done of members and providers are not aligned in the US health care system.

At some health care providers, such as Intermountain Health-care, Kaiser Permanente, and Geisinger Health System, managers are aggressively working to align the jobs of providers and the consumers in their care. One of the most important ways they do this is by assuming responsibility for the cost of care—by insuring consumers, for instance. The organizations' financial sustainability therefore depends on keeping consumers as healthy as possible over the course of their relationship with providers; and this dependency enables jobs-focused innovation around disease prevention, and care efficiency and effectiveness, to flourish. It enables providers to focus on keeping consumers healthy, instead of waiting until they get sick to step in; and on helping them get well as soon as possible, or effectively managing chronic conditions, when they do get sick. The result? The jobs of the provider and consumer are aligned well.

These plans are in stark contrast to traditional plans, in which providers are paid only for specific services delivered to consumers. In this context, providers have no financial incentive to keep consumers healthy over the long term or to manage the cost of care delivery—and they have every incentive to increase the volume of care delivered. Their jobs and consumers' jobs are painfully misaligned.

In Our Lives

What job do we elect a political leader to do for us and our nation? What job do *they think* we are hiring them to do and how does that compare with the job *we think* we're hiring them to do when we go into the voting booth? Are they aligned? Are we hiring people to lead us? Or to give voice to our fears? They're not the same thing. As I mentioned in chapter 8, Peter Drucker famously cautioned us: "The customer rarely buys what the company thinks it is selling him." I suspect there's a profound disconnect between voters and politicians, too, and that's why we're continually dissatisfied with the people we elect to serve us.

Think about this disconnect the next time you go to church, synagogue, or another house of worship—or deliberately *don't* go. The Jobs to Be Done Theory explains why so many churches are struggling to keep their members. They have lost a sense for the jobs that arise in their members' lives, for which they might hire a church.

I could go on for hours about how the Theory of Jobs helps us see the world in unique and insightful ways. Good theories are not meant to teach us *what* to think. Rather, they teach us *how* to think. I encourage you to continue the conversation from here in your home or your office after you put this book down.

HOW THEORY HELPS *YOU*

A few years ago, in the middle of the class I teach at Harvard— "Building and Sustaining a Successful Enterprise" (BSSE)—one of my students raised her hand to ask a question. We were about halfway through the semester and, as usual, we had spent our time learning various theories that I believe are the most import- ant tools I can give my students before they venture out in the world. I've gotten a *lot* of questions over the years, and I'm usually prepared for anything. But this one threw me a bit. "Excuse me, professor. I don't mean to be rude, but I wanted to know what's the *purpose* of this course?" I was surprised because I thought it was clear that we were preparing them to accomplish great things in their careers and personal lives and to navigate the difficult decisions that would inevitably come their way. But I asked her if I could think about it overnight. The next day I had an answer that not only satisfied her, but satisfied me: "In this class we learn theories that explain *what causes what to happen.* Isn't it great to know how things work?"

That has been the aim of this book, too. If you know how innovation works—what truly causes innovation to succeed—your efforts don't have to be left to fate. We've allowed ourselves to believe that luck is essential for far too long. There are whole industries, such as venture capital, that are currently organized around the belief that innovation is essentially a game of playing the odds. But it's time to topple that tired paradigm. I've spent twenty years gathering evidence so that you can put your time, energy, and resources into creating products and services that you *can predict,* in advance, customers will be eager to hire. Leave relying on luck to the other guys.

NOTES

1. Johnson, H. Thomas, and Robert S. Kaplan. *Relevance Lost: The Rise and Fall of Management Accounting.* Boston: Harvard Business School Press, 1987.

2. Christensen, Clayton M., James Allworth, and Karen Dillon. *How Will You Measure Your Life?* New York: HarperCollins, 2012.

3. Christensen, Clayton M., Michael B. Horn, and Curtis W. Johnson. *Disrupting Class: How Disruptive Innovation Will Change the Way the World Learns.* New York: McGraw-Hill, 2008.

4. We know of at least five authors who have published books named *Hidden in Plain Sight.* They are Jan Chipchase and Simon Steinhardt, Erich Joachimsthaler, Andrew H. Thomas, and Peter J. Wallison. We thank them, and undoubtedly others, with this marvelous phrase that we shamelessly borrow in this chapter.

5. Christensen, Clayton M., Jerome H. Grossman, and Jason Hwang. *The Innovator's Prescription: A Disruptive Solution for Health Care.* New York: McGraw-Hill Education, 2009.

ACKNOWLEDGMENTS

FROM CLAYTON CHRISTENSEN

It took eight years to develop the Theory of Disruptive Innovation and write the book that explains it, *The Innovator's Dilemma*. In contrast, it has taken us nearly *two decades* to hone the Jobs to Be Done Theory of marketing that we summarize in this book. What explains the difference? I had a treasure trove of data about disk drives, which yielded the theory of disruption. We had no such luck with our Jobs Theory research. We had to collect the data person by person, company by company. There have been no short cuts.

For these reasons, I am deeply indebted to many people who have helped me develop this body of theory that describes an important cause of successful innovation. Two decades ago Bob Moesta first walked into my office at Harvard Business School with a lot of questions. He'd read my theory of disruption and was eager to apply it in his own consulting business to help his clients. I don't think either one of us would have guessed at that first meeting that it would be the beginning of a long conversation—and collaboration. It was Bob and his partner Rick Pedi who first brought me the puzzle that eventually led to the Theory of Jobs to Be Done and his work in the years since has helped shape it. Bob and I have met faithfully once a quarter for twenty years, and I don't think I've ever left a meeting without learning something from him. An engineer by training, early on in his career he had the good fortune to be mentored by both

Dr. Genichi Taguchi and W. Edwards Deming. It is his work applying and shaping Jobs Theory that has been the basis of our own fruitful partnership. I encouraged him to set up a consulting firm—the Re-Wired Group—to use Jobs Theory on difficult innovation challenges for his clients, and I introduced him and this theory to Innosight, a consultancy that I helped start. I've also brought him into my classroom many times to demonstrate Jobs Theory in action. I can think of no better ambassador for jobs. Watching him interview a random volunteer from the audience is like watching a magician at work—I never fail to be amazed at what he elicits. I'm grateful for our years of collaboration—and, more important, our enduring friendship.

Intuit cofounder Scott Cook has been very engaged in Jobs Theory for years. His thinking helped shape the theory in the early years and he and I, together with this book's coauthor Taddy Hall, wrote the first article on Jobs Theory in *Harvard Business Review* in 2005. After numerous conversations about how the theory applied to his own company, Scott helped me understand that there are a lot of "negative jobs"—jobs that people simply do not want to have to do. I've learned a lot from talking to Scott and his employees at Intuit over the years, including how challenging it is to keep an organization focused on customers' jobs. We owe a lot of our insights to Scott and his teams.

In building theories, I have learned that finding skeptics with have something worthwhile to say is invaluable. Michael Christensen, a Baker Scholar and Harvard Business School graduate who also happens to be my son, has fit this role selflessly. I don't know how many evenings Michael and I debated the boundaries and explanatory power of the Jobs Theory. He is not cynical. Rather, he has very high standards of intellectual integrity in his pursuit of truth. His pushback helped us make the theory much better. I'm grateful for his courage to stand up to his dad. Jobs Theory is stronger and better as a result.

Dave Sundahl has worked with me for years, most recently as a senior research fellow at the Christensen Institute. David knows more than anyone I've met about how robust theories must be built. He can smell a charlatan before he finishes its first paragraph, and knows which scholars of theory can and cannot be trusted. I'm grateful for his help in putting boundaries around the Theory of Jobs. I think he loves a good theory as much as I do, but he's relentless about making sure it's sound before we share it with the world.

Led by my insightful and articulate colleague Derek van Bever, annually we invite a few of our best graduating students to become fellows in the Forum for Innovation and Growth at Harvard Business School. These truly are the best of the best, and they join with us for one or two additional years to develop, improve, and disseminate theories about innovation and management. Max Wessel put his career on hold to shape and advance our thinking about Jobs Theory and its application during his two years at the forum. His contribution helped make Jobs Theory stronger and more useful for managers in the real world. He has continued to be a valuable voice and a true friend and I'm grateful for his contribution. Laura Day spent a year with the forum advancing our thinking and helping the team understand better how to uncover jobs in the real world—and her shear enthusiasm for the subject made every conversation or debate not only productive, but a pleasure for me as well. Tom Bartman, Efosa Ojomo, James Allworth, Dina Wang, and Jason Orgill also helped us understand how Jobs Theory interacts with other models of management that they were developing.

The field of jobs has benefited greatly from the thinking and fieldwork of my colleagues at Innosight over the years, in particular, Managing Partner Scott Anthony, who hammered out with me some of the most fundamental concepts of the theory. He has been a trusted thought partner and friend. Senior Partner Joe Sinfield also made significant contributions to the theory by pioneering its use in major corporations. Innosight's work with Fortune 100 clients has pushed the envelope on how to get an entire corporation to embrace the concept of jobs, build it systematically into the activities of brand teams and businesses, and get executives at different levels to understand how jobs insights drive strategic and tactical decisions.

My teaching colleagues—Derek van Bever, Chet Huber, Stephen Kaufman, Rory McDonald, Willy Shih, Raj Choudhury, and Ray Gilmartin—are some of the smartest and most selfless people in the world. Every day they use our theories to explore how to solve problems and create growth opportunities for companies. But they also find situations or outcomes that our research cannot yet explain and then help me resolve these anomalies and improve the theories. I tutored each of them in how to teach my MBA course, and now they tutor me on how to teach my course. I am grateful to have the opportunity to work with people of this caliber.

There were many others who shared important insights along the way. Mike Collins, founder and CEO of the BIG Idea Group (BIG), was one of the first CEOs I know of to use the jobs idea very effectively. Gerald Berstell and Denise Nitterhouse coauthored one of my early articles on Jobs Theory and played an important role in shaping and sharing our early vision.

Nitin Nohria, the dean of Harvard Business School, has played a critical role in cultivating a climate of inquiry at HBS. He has supported the Forum for Innovation and Growth, which is helping us stay in touch intellectually with about seventy-five hundred alumni of my course, "Building and Sustaining a Successful Enterprise." Just as they did when they were in our classrooms, the alumni of BSSE continue to find anomalies that our theories cannot yet explain; and they use the theories from the course to create companies—many of them very successful companies! I am proud of them.

My colleagues at the Christensen Institute have done the same—asked and sought answers for some of the most important questions facing organizations today. I regard them as knights around our round table. They each left blossoming careers to join me in researching the problems of management.

And now to my dream team. I am blessed to have been able to work with Taddy Hall, Karen Dillon, and Dave Duncan on this book. Taddy was a student in my first-ever class at HBS. I can still picture him in the top row right on the aisle between the left and center sections. Taddy and I collaborated several times over the years, perhaps most notably coauthoring the first Jobs Theory article in *Harvard Business Review*. I have turned to Taddy because he always manages to bring a healthy dose of real-world experience—and healthy skepticism—combined with genuine zeal for the theories to our discussions. I've come to deeply value his sharp mind, his ability to pull interesting parallels and examples into our conversations, and his good humor and laughter.

Karen Dillon is among the best writers and editors on earth. She and I have collaborated twice, on this book and on *How Will You Measure Your Life?* Her skill in translating academic thinking to something that practitioners can genuinely understand and use in their everyday lives is apparent on each page. I'm grateful for her tireless enthusiasm and energizing spirit in navigating the challenges of writing a book worth reading. But she's been more than a writer on this project; she's been an invaluable thought partner, collaborator, and friend. I truly feel sorry for anyone who doesn't have the opportunity to work with Karen.

Over the past decade, David Duncan's work in helping to develop and implement Jobs Theory has made him one of its most knowledgeable and innovative practitioners I know. As a senior partner in Innosight, he's worked with a host of global companies as they work their way through difficult innovation and growth challenges and I know Dave's work has had a lasting impact. He's had that same effect on our thinking in this book, as we've worked through some difficult nuances and challenges in understanding and explaining Jobs Theory. Long before Dave began to think about innovation, he earned his PhD in physics at Harvard—and I was the beneficiary of that trained analytical mind in all of our interactions.

Although convention is not to list them as coauthors, we could not have completed this book without Emily Snyder and Jon Palmer. Both contribute not only to the quality of our lives, but also to the quality of our work. Emily has been my right arm for five years and I can't think of a single day that she did not tackle with sheer enthusiasm to make the world a better place. In interactions both big and small, she makes a difference to everyone who comes into contact with this office. I knew when I hired Jon that he'd be an asset to our team. But I had no idea just how much—and how quickly. Not only has he gotten up to speed about the complex array of theories, people, and projects in this office, but he's contributed—significantly—to them as well. I've come to count on his sharp mind, his boundless energy, and perhaps most of all, his good judgment.

I have made capable colleagues and lifelong friends through this process. I will never be able to thank them enough for being willing to work alongside me every day.

My agent, Danny Stern, has provided able assistance with some of my most important projects for nearly twenty years, with the support of his colleagues Kristen Soehngen Karp and Ned Ward. I'm grateful both for their sound guidance and for their commitment to ensuring that the values that we share are part of our work together. Our editor for this book, Hollis Heimbouch, has been a valued partner for many years. Her rare ability to both support and push me, her deft editing touch, and her belief in the power of great ideas has been a source of inspiration for our whole team.

Most of all, I'm grateful for a wonderful team at home—our children Matthew, Ann, Michael, Spencer, and Katie Christensen. They have questioned, tested, edited, and used every paragraph of this book. Our children now have their own careers. My wife, Christine, and I are proud of their success—in part because they have used the theories about management that were honed in discussions at home. Beyond this, however, Christine and I are most proud that every day they remember why God sent us to this earth. We taught this to them. Now our children, their spouses, and our grandchildren teach this to us. For this we eternally will be grateful. And most of all, I thank my wife, Christine, whose insightful thoughts and deft editing touch are present explicitly or implicitly on every page of this book. I can't think of a better life partner and I'm humbled and grateful that she's mine.

—*Clayton Christensen*

FROM TADDY HALL

It's nothing profound to note that the big stuff in life tends to show up unannounced, unexpected, and, certainly in the case of my long friendship with Clay Christensen, undeserved.

Twenty-four years ago when I walked into the classroom for the first day of Clay's class, I had no idea of the adventure that was about to begin. Over these many years, there has never been a conversation with Clay that didn't leave me feeling a humbled sense of gratitude for his patience, wisdom, and kindness. Thank you, Clay.

I also want to thank coauthors Karen and Dave. Dave's mind works with a logical precision that I envy—providing order to complex ideas, and he has made this book much, much better. If there's anyone in the world thinking of ever writing a book, I just hope that there's a Karen Dillon in your life. Many times I felt like the fortuitous shoemaker leaving ratty cloth out by night only to awake to find a glorious pair of shoes on the workbench. That's what working with Karen is like.

Jon Palmer, Clay's chief of staff, joined the team mid-season and never missed a beat. If you're lucky, you've had a "day I met Jon Palmer" moment in your life: a fresh face enters the fray and within minutes you're wondering, "How did we ever function without him?" Jon had this instant effect on our team: making his presence felt by gently making everything we did better, easier, and more fun.

Should you ever send Clay an email, you'll receive an instant response stating that "Emily Snyder runs my world." This is both true and a blessing; indeed, after years of working with Clay and Emily, I only wish Emily would run my world as well.

Friends and colleagues have been amazingly generous and indispensably wise: Herb Allen, Bob Barocci, Barry Calpino, Scott Cook, Mike DePanfilis, Craig Dubitsky, Barry Goldblatt, Jason Green, Brian Halligan, Rod Hogan, Steve Hughes, Larry Keeley, Jim Kilts, Peter Klein, Stace Lindsay, Sheila Marcelo, Pete Maulik, Pat McGauley, Tom Monahan, Parker Noren, Diego Piacentini, Michael Raynor, Saul Rosenberg, Jennifer Saenz, Rogelio de los Santos, Anshu Sharma, Geoff Tanner, Jay Walker, Mike Wege, Rob Wengel, Eddie Yoon, Jerry Zaltman.

I am grateful, daily, to my innovation colleagues at the Nielsen Company and the Cambridge Group for the many opportunities to apply our ideas in the real world.

Eduardo Salazar and his team have created a real-world laboratory to test our theories and create new growth businesses in Colombia. Eduardo proves that the intersection of innovation and insanity can be a wildly productive place.

Several years ago, Ann Christensen and I collaborated on a series of projects involving high-growth companies in emerging markets. Ann sharpened my thinking and improved many of our ideas. She's made this book better.

Anyone who wonders whether innovation can not only change the world but maybe even save it should meet Linda Rottenberg and the team at Endeavor. For twenty years Linda has been a friend and inspiration. Working with Linda and the thousand-plus high-impact entrepreneurs comprising the Endeavor Network has enabled us to apply and improve our theories in every conceivable industry and cultural context.

Erich Joachimsthaler of the Vivaldi Group is both a great friend and an invaluable thought partner. Many times over recent years, Erich has taken time away from his amazing work to sort out and strengthen my incomplete, half-formed thoughts.

Bob Moesta has done as much to develop Jobs Theory as anyone—and he's a brother to me.

The first and most accomplished innovator I've known was my grandfather and best friend, Dwight E. Harken. He was a natural innovator who changed the world. Told that the human heart was too complicated for surgical intervention, he sensed that the real problem was that the heart was poorly understood. He went on to pioneer the field of heart surgery, opening the field by removing shrapnel from 130 World War II soldiers without a fatality. Later, on seeing many patients survive risky surgical procedures only to succumb in the ward, he applied Jobs Theory decades before we'd thought of it. By integrating across diverse medical functions, he created the world's first intensive care unit, saving untold numbers of lives as a consequence.

I imagine a few hermits have written books, but for the rest of us it is often an uninvited family enterprise. My wife, Karen, and our daughters, Penelope and Hadley, have made untold sacrifices for a book that's unlikely to top their Christmas wish lists. But they have given me the greatest gifts of all: a life of meaning, love, and laughter. The book took some time from us, so let's go play.

—*Taddy Hall*

FROM KAREN DILLON

One of the best parts about getting a call from Clay Christensen is that it always leads to something unexpected, interesting, and inspiring. This book was no exception. I consider myself privileged to have had the chance to collaborate again with a man who is brilliant, kind, and generous not some of the time, not much of the time, but *all* of the time. The fact that he also happens to be a world-class thought leader is just the icing on the cake. The opportunity to work closely with you, Clay, is a gift that I do not take for granted.

I didn't know either of my coauthors, Taddy Hall and Dave Duncan, until Clay put us together to work on this book, but how lucky am I that he did. In the many days, weeks, and months of throwing our hearts and souls into this book, there was not a single moment that I wasn't grateful that you were my partners. Taddy, I still can't quite figure out when you slept during a stretch of months, but your commitment, your insight, and your enthusiasm for doing great work never waned. And Dave, your depth and breadth of knowledge about jobs in the real world is simply spectacular—and you have the gift of being able to explain and share complex ideas in powerful, understandable ways. I've learned so much from both of you.

Emily Snyder and Jon Palmer, there aren't enough words to tell you how grateful I am that you were our partners on this book. You have both been present and supportive in more ways than I dared hope for—and done so entirely selflessly. Emily, you blew into my life like a ray of sunshine and constantly lifted my spirits. Jon, in spite of joining the party late, you immediately became indispensable. Is there anything you're *not* great at doing? I've yet to find out. You were both my rocks.

I can't think of a single one of our numerous conversations with Bob Moesta that didn't start with him offering: "How can I help?" Bob's thinking, his experience, and his ideas—all of which he offered freely—are deeply embedded throughout this book. Watching Bob do a jobs interview is seeing a master at the peak of his craft. I hope with this book we've managed to shine a bit more light on your genius.

I feel incredibly lucky to have had the insightful minds of the Forum for Growth and Innovation and the Christensen Institute at my disposal. I'd like to particularly thank Derek van Bever and Laura Day—who went out of their ways to help in any way I asked. Tom Bartman, Efosa Ojomo, Max Wessel, and Tracy Horn each provided support along the way. The Christensen Institute's brilliant David Sundahl was a true partner, freely and enthusiastically spending hours working through the theory with us. I am grateful for Ann Christensen, Rebecca Fogg, and our intrepid fact checker Michael Devonas, who each helped me navigate challenges in the course of writing this book. I am also, once again, indebted to the top-notch team from Stern Strategy Group, Danny Stern, Kristen Soehngen Karp, and Ania Trzepizur, as well as our editor at HarperCollins, Hollis Heimbouch, whose enthusiastic encouragement and expert guidance always provide just the right balance of support and inspiration, and to her right hand on this project, Stephanie Hitchcock, you have been a terrific ally.

I want to thank Paul LeBlanc and his team at Southern New Hampshire University, Chet Huber, Scott Cook, Pleasant Rowland, Clark Gilbert, Bob Whitman, Ethan Bernstein, Todd Dunn and his team at Intermountain, Chip Conley, Sal Khan, David Goulait, Apple's John Couch, Intercom's Des Traynor and Eoghan McCabe, Precision Nutrition's Phil Caravaggio, and SC Johnson's Lauren Lackey for their generosity of time and spirit in embracing our thinking and sharing their stories with us. You helped us bring these ideas to life.

My own kitchen cabinet included friends and colleagues past and present and I am grateful to have such thoughtful and generous people to turn to. Rajesh Bilimoria was both patient and inspiring as he spent hours discussing jobs with me. James Allworth is always there when I need him. Innosight's Scott Anthony offered rapid and insightful feedback. Mallory Dwinal thoughtfully responded without hesitation to my endless stream of queries. I'm grateful that James de Vries, my gifted *HBR* colleague, put his hand up to help. My virtual colleagues, Jane Heifetz and Amy Gallo, have kept me both sane and laughing throughout this project.

And most important of all, the reason I am able to spend endless hours working on projects that challenge me to grow is my family. To my daughters, Rebecca and Emma: you have encouraged me to never stop pursuing professional dreams while inspiring me to always put my personal ones first. To my beloved mother, Marilyn Dillon, who has read every word of this book—and every other important writing project in my life—with her eagle eye, I once again thank you for caring about my work as much as I do. And finally, my best friend and husband, Richard. There's so much to thank you for: for literally being by my side for hundreds of hours of conversations for this book; for being my most devoted idea scout; for providing intelligent food for thought and constructive criticism; for silently placing cups of tea on my desk at just the right moments; and for patiently listening without ever giving the slightest hint that you might be "full" of jobs talk. This book is a reflection of your unconditional support and I would never have been able to do this without you.

—*Karen Dillon*

FROM DAVID S. DUNCAN

I feel very fortunate to have been involved in the creation of this book from the ground up. This would not have been possible without the support of Clay Christensen, whom I have had the good fortune to know and work with since I joined Innosight twelve years ago. I have always greatly admired not only his ability to come up with powerful new ideas, but also his extraordinary gifts as a teacher, writer, and storyteller. He's also one of the kindest and most generous people I've known. I'm very grateful to have had this opportunity to work with him on such an exciting project.

Our wonderful team has made writing this book both rewarding and enjoyable. My other coauthors, Karen Dillon and Taddy Hall, were a genuine pleasure to work with. Karen is a fantastic writer and storyteller, one of the nicest and smartest people I know, and she held the team together and kept us on track throughout the project. Taddy was a consistent source of fresh insights and interesting stories drawn from his extensive experience, and we all benefited from his great sense of humor. Our core team included Jon Palmer, Emily Snyder, and Tara Goss, who contributed in innumerable ways and provided wisdom and positive energy throughout.

Although I was the Innosight partner who worked on this book, I viewed my role as not just contributing my own ideas but also channeling some of the terrific work and ideas developed by other Innosight colleagues over the years. Joe Sinfield and Scott Anthony played a big role in developing some of the foundational thinking about jobs, and in developing the myriad ways it can be applied and institutionalized in large organizations. I've also benefited greatly from the many discussions I've had over the years with Andy Waldeck, Mark Johnson, and more recently Patrick Viguerie. Cathy Olofson and Evan Schwartz provided wise counsel and many great ideas based on their deep expertise in editing, writing, and marketing. I'm very grateful to be part of the leadership team of such an inspiring organization.

Many clients and former colleagues I've worked with over the years have shaped my thinking on jobs, but I owe a special thanks to those who contributed their time and stories to this book. In particular, thanks to Jacques Goulet, Keyne Monson, Dave Goulait, and Hari Nair for being generous with their time and patiently working with us to tell their important and inspiring stories.

I owe the greatest debt of gratitude to my wonderful family. My parents and brother Brian have always and without fail supported me regardless of the divergent paths I've taken, which has made all the difference throughout my life. I'd also like to thank my Rhode Island family, Ed, Claire, and Christine, for their love and support. Above all I'm deeply grateful to my wife, Suzanne, and my daughter, Zoe, who never fail to make me smile, inspire me, give me purpose, and remind me what matters most. I dedicate my portion of this book to them.

—*David S. Duncan*

INDEX

Pages numbers followed by n indicate notes.

CLAYTON M. CHRISTENSEN is the Kim B. Clark Professor at Harvard Business School, the author of nine books, a five-time recipient of the McKinsey Award for *Harvard Business Review*'s best article, and the cofounder of four companies, including the innovation consulting firm Innosight. In 2011 and 2013 he was named the world's most influential business thinker in a biennial ranking conducted by Thinkers50.

TADDY HALL is a principal with the Cambridge Group and a leader of Nielsen's Breakthrough Innovation project. In these capacities, he helps senior executives create successful new products and improve innovation processes. He also works extensively with executives in emerging markets as an adviser to Endeavor and Innovation Without Borders.

KAREN DILLON is the former editor of the *Harvard Business Review* and coauthor of the *New York Times* bestseller *How Will You Measure Your Life?* She is a graduate of Cornell University and Northwestern University's Medill School of Journalism. In 2011 she was named by Ashoka as one of the world's most influential and inspiring women.

DAVID S. DUNCAN is a senior partner at Innosight. He's a leading thinker and adviser to senior executives on innovation strategy and growth, helping them navigate disruptive change, create sustainable growth, and transform their organizations to thrive for the long term. He is a graduate of Duke University and earned a PhD in physics from Harvard University.

ALSO BY CLAYTON CHRISTENSEN

HOW WILL YOU MEASURE YOUR LIFE?
by Clayton M. Christensen,
James Allworth & Karen Dillon
Available in Hardcover, Digital Audio, and E-book

"Recommend the book to friends and family who have no connection to the business world. They will thank you for it." —*Harvard Business Review*

In this groundbreaking book, Christensen puts forth a series of questions: How can I be sure that I'll find satisfaction in my career? How can I be sure that my personal relationships become enduring sources of happiness? How can I avoid compromising my integrity—and stay out of jail? Using lessons from some of the world's greatest businesses, he provides incredible insights into these challenging questions.

How Will You Measure Your Life? is full of inspiration and wisdom, and will help students, midcareer professionals, and parents alike forge their own paths to fulfillment.